FACING THE FRONTIER

THE STORY OF
THE MACGREGOR RANCH

Betty D. Freudenburg

Betty D. Freudenburg

Published by the
Rocky Mountain Nature Association

Made possible by a grant from the
Colorado Endowment for the Hu

Published by the
Rocky Mountain Nature Association
Rocky Mountain National Park
Estes Park, CO 80517

Library of Congress Catalog Card Number 98-67787
ISBN: 0-930487-97-4

Printed in the United States of America

Project director/editor: John Gunn
Editor: Erin Turner
Design: Ann Green
Front cover photo: *MacGregor Ranch Foreman Mitch Brown enjoys the view of
Longs Peak before beginning another day of work. (James Frank)*
Back cover photo: *Majestic snowcapped mountains and lush, grass-filled
pastures lure visitors to the historical MacGregor Ranch. (Mary Ann Kressig)*

To MacGregor Ranch
volunteers, staff, directors and visitors.
That we all may know
Alexander and Clara better.

Twin Owls along Lumpy Ridge in Rocky Mountain National Park provides a scenic backdrop for Estes Park's MacGregor Ranch. (John Gunn)

TABLE OF CONTENTS

ACKNOWLEDGMENTS

*M*ore than 10 years have passed since this MacGregor Ranch volunteer offered to transcribe the fragile 1875-1877 diaries of Alexander and Clara MacGregor. I will be forever grateful to the host of librarians, historical society and museum staff members, friends and even chance acquaintances whose names are not included here, but whose encouragement and kind deeds during that time will not be forgotten.

Thanks go out to Curt Buchholtz, executive director of the Rocky Mountain Nature Association, for his inquiries, suggestions and manuscript review; Bill Gwaltney and the Rocky Mountain National Park interpretive staff for their reviews; David Wetzel for his exceptional guidance and for encouraging me to apply for a grant from the Colorado Endowment for the Humanities; Rebecca Lintz for introducing me to the Alva Adams Collection #2 in the archives of the Colorado Historical Society; Stan Oliner for suggesting that the diaries might possibly be microfilmed – not *if* I finished, but *when*; and Clark Secrest for his requests to quote from Alva Adams' anonymous travel columns I had discovered in the *Black Earth Advertiser*.

What a privilege it has been to be able to consult with Jim Pickering, and to accept his offer to use his unpublished book *This Blue Hollow: The Annals of Estes Park: A Colorado Reader* for reference purposes. Gladys Thomson and Harriet Burgess were indispensable, and seemed never to tire of helping whenever asked. Lorna Knowlton was very supportive. Ferrel Atkins offered welcomed assistance, as did Lennie Bemiss of the Estes Park Public Library, Lynn Swain and Lisel Goetze of the Estes Park Area Historical Museum and archivist Bea Malchow with the Longmont Public Library.

Hydrologist George Clausen was very helpful by describing how Alex MacGregor's sawmill utilized the Black Canyon Creek to power the mill's turbine. Also deserving much credit is engineer-surveyor Bill Van Horn, who reconstructed a map of the toll road MacGregor built between the Estes Park and Lyons vicinities.

John Gunn, publications director for the Rocky Mountain Nature Association, was extremely helpful in coordinating this project from pre-planning to production and printing. He also was inspired to contribute photographs and create three of the maps in this book. Thanks to both John and fellow editor Erin Turner, Helena, Montana, for their meticulous, invaluable organizing and editing skills, and to Ann Green for her efforts as designer of this book.

Those most responsible for solving the mystery of Alexander MacGregor's ancestry were Assistant Chieftan Joseph C. Tichy Jr. of the American Clan Gregor Society, Whispering Pines, North Carolina; Barney Bloom, Vermont Historical

Society, Montpelier, Vermont; and Duncan B. McGregor, Gibbon, Nebraska.

Mention must also be made of Tom Noel's interest and encouragement, Joanne Ditmer's inspiration and truly appreciated critique and Marshall Sprague's personal note and helpful advice in answer to my letter.

In Pueblo, I was fortunate in being able to consult with Ed Broadhead, Edward Simonich, Alva B. Adams III, Librarian Helene Spitzer of the *Pueblo Chieftan* (formerly the *Star-Journal*) and Stina Stjernholm, reference librarian, University Southern Colorado. Staff was very helpful at Alamosa's Adams State College Library and Boulder's Norlin and Carnegie libraries. Peggy Ford offered indispensable help at the Greeley Museums. Wilbur Ball of Eaton, Colorado, and Martha Thompson of Pine Bluffs, Wyoming, reviewed the probable trail taken by the Adams family from Julesburg to Pine Bluffs to Greeley. Credit is also due Anne Matlack, Mary Meining and Dwight Webster of Longmont; Don Meining of Platteville; Verlene Thorp and Marlene Kanok of Pinewood Springs; and LaVern M. Johnson of the Lyons Historical Society.

Colorado Springs was a rich source of relevant historical information. Special thanks should be given to the archivist at the *Gazette Telegraph*, as well as to Rhoda Wilcox for consulting with me in her home. Thanks also go to Ginny Kiefer and Robin Satterwhite, Tutt Library, Colorado College, and the helpful staffs at the Starsmore Center for Local History at the Pioneers Museum and the Local History Room of the Penrose Library.

Persons from Wisconsin who helped bring this project to fruition are James Hansen, reference librarian, State Historical Society, Madison; Paul Woehrmann, Local History and Marine Collection, and Sandy Broder, Great Lakes Marine Collection, Milwaukee Public Library; Nicholas L. Neylon, Milwaukee Urban Archives, the Golda Meir Library, University of Wisconsin-Milwaukee; Timothy D. Cary, archdiocesan archivist, Archdiocese of Milwaukee; Sister Alice Lechnir, archivist, School Sisters of Notre Dame, Milwaukee; Eleanor Carrier and Nancy Durgin, Albion Academy Historical Society, Edgerton; Virgil Matz, research historian, Black Earth and Mazomanie; Robert Dodsworth, Mazomanie Historical Society; and Raymond M. Virnig, Cross Plains-Berry Historical Society. Valuable assistance was received at these additional Wisconsin institutions: Milwaukee County Historical Society, Oconomowoc Historical Society, Waukesha County Museum, Blanchardville Public Library and at the University of Wisconsin-Madison, the archives, alumni association and Memorial Library.

Thanks to a grant from the Colorado Endowment for the Humanities, extended research was possible in Chicago, Milwaukee, Madison and Black Earth, in addition to Denver, Colorado Springs and Pueblo. Mention must also be made of the telephone consultations with Griff Evans' grandson, Richard Evans of Carson City, Nevada. But the author's greatest indebtedness is to each member of her family for their forbearance and calm endurance.

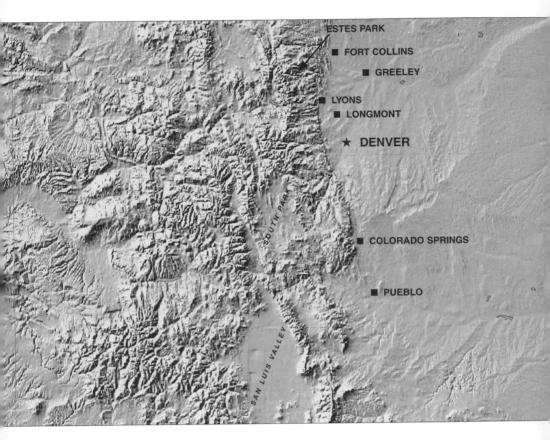

Alva, Alex & Clara's Colorado. (Relief map courtesy of Ray Sterner, Johns Hopkins University

INTRODUCTION

*F*ew eras in American history loom so large in our national consciousness as the great westward expansion, particularly the days of the "Old West." The Old West actually existed for only a quarter of a century, between the end of the Civil War in 1865 and roughly 1890, when the United States Census Bureau declared that the frontier was no more. In those few decades, the settling of the West was completed, and the myths and images of the West that have settled so deeply into the American psyche were created.

Perhaps because of the thousands of stories and movies that have emerged about the legends of that era, we know much more about the fictional heroes of the Old West than the real ones. However, what happened to western heroes in real life often is as compelling as fiction. Today, as writer Richard Wheeler once claimed, people are yearning for "a more realistic story, about real people challenging the awesome difficulties posed by the Wild West." Wrote Wheeler:

> *The real historical West offers far better material, more colorful and fantastic, than the wildest imaginings of the romantic western novelists. For a brief, unique period in the 19th century, the great western expansion into unknown lands fraught with dangers captured the imagination of the country — indeed, of the world. There had never been anything like it, and never will be again. Far from being exhausted and arid as a result of innumerable western novels, films and TV series, the real frontier West is virtually untouched, virginal material. . . . The traditional mythic western has used this material only as backdrop or stage setting while focusing on its real theme: male pecking-order*

Alva Adams.

Alexander MacGregor.

Clara Heeney.

struggles between loners on a lawless land where the social rules didn't apply. But the real West was rarely like that. The real stories and characters are much wilder, more violent, more astonishing than anything on the paperback racks.[1]

The experiences of Colorado's early pioneers may or may not have been astonishing, but they certainly are worthy of attention. This book will discuss the lives of three settlers from Wisconsin: Alva Adams, Alexander MacGregor and Clara Heeney. When they emigrated to the Colorado Territory, Wisconsin was emerging from its own frontier era. This trio of pioneers exemplified and contributed to Colorado's own "real historical West." Their lives are of interest to us in their own right, but the record of their experiences also illustrates some of the changes that were taking place during the frontier era.

Within a half dozen years of the end of the Civil War, wooden sidewalks were being built in the city of Denver, Colorado Territory. The city's two-mile-long, horse-drawn railway was becoming the preferred method of transport for hundreds of former pedestrians; ox-pulled wagon trains, stages and six-horse coaches were being replaced by locomotives; and this fast-growing community was elated over the installation of gaslights and the progress of the waterworks. Optimistic residents predicted that Denver would be the capital of the United States within 50 years.

It was in the midst of this bustle, on October 10, 1871, that the *Rocky Mountain News* carried the story of a young man destined for fame. The newspaper reported that Alva Adams was busy in Colorado Springs setting up shop for the new Sanborn and Adams lumberyard and constructing a one-story building, 24 feet by 80 feet, where customers would select from a general assortment of builder's material, furniture and other merchandise.

The same issue of the paper contained two other apparently unrelated front-page stories. One item was a simple mention that a man named Alexander Q. MacGregor was being considered for jury duty. The other was one of the biggest news stories of the 19th century: Much of the city of Chicago, Illinois, had just burned. Not mentioned in the story of the fire was a young woman of 19 who happened to be in Chicago at the time. Her name was Clara Heeney, and she was an artist. Clara was Alva Adams' childhood sweetheart, but she would become A.Q. MacGregor's bride.

Clara Heeney, Alva Adams and Alex MacGregor all were raised in a time when a state was beginning to emerge from the Territory of Wisconsin, when Wisconsin, not Colorado, was part of the far-western frontier. Two of the three became well known after they moved to Colorado. In 1887, at age 36, Alva Adams became the governor of Colorado. Also in the 1880s, Alexander MacGregor became prominent as one of the first residents of Estes Park, Colorado, where he and his wife founded Black Canyon Ranch, now known as the MacGregor Ranch.

In the past, little has been said about the early lives of these important young residents, or about how their lives were interrelated. The three pioneers were engulfed by the waves of tumult and change that were sweeping across the young nation. They struggled with the issues of Indians and agriculture, temperance and tuberculosis, suffrage and suffering. In the process, they left records that help us gain a better sense of the influences on their lives and the effects all three had on their environments.

In writing *Facing the Frontier,* I used three main source materials. The first is a series of love letters written by Alva to Clara in their youth. These convey the lonely heartaches of a young man torn from his home and his beloved.

The second source is the *Black Earth Advertiser,* the newspaper of Black Earth, Wisconsin, hometown of Clara and Alva. The paper carried news stories about the western exploits of the Adams and Heeney families, as well as travel and opinion columns penned by an anonymous writer using the nom de plume "Dane." In the course of writing this book, the author discovered that Dane was actually Alva Adams. Alva apparently wished to remain anonymous in his correspondences. His Dane articles carried the strong opinions and tenor of a future governor, and they stood in sharp contrast to his more heartfelt love letters.[2]

The third principal source area includes the diaries of Alex and Clara MacGregor, Clara's autograph album and scrapbook, and other memorabilia. I acquired access to these while working as a volunteer at the historical MacGregor Ranch. I offered to transcribe the MacGregors' 1875-1877 diaries, which were difficult to read and becoming quite fragile. Their entries covered the most crucial period of time in the development of their ranch. They touched on the roles the MacGregors played in the early history of Estes Park and provide a fresh look at pioneer life on the western frontier.

One other source of significance is the Alva Adams Collection Number 2 from the archives of the Colorado Historical Society.[3] Miscellaneous additional sources include a wealth of other archival material at locations in Colorado, Wyoming, Wisconsin and Illinois. I also have been in contact with the great grandson of the governor, Alva B. Adams III, who lives in Pueblo; the grandson of an important MacGregor ranch hand; the grandson of Estes Park pioneer Griffith J. Evans; and descendants of the MacGregors.

This volume is an effort to provide an account of the early days of three westerners, to correct some of the anomalies and blind spots of past research and to bring into focus the kinds of real human experiences of the Old West which much to our detriment, have long been forgotten.

The order of the letters, some undated, was determined by the events mentioned therein. Although the *Advertiser's* printers' errors could have been responsible for some of the mistakes recorded in this manuscript, every effort has been made to remain faithful to the original letters, diaries and newspaper accounts concerning Alva, Clara and Alex, and to make as few changes as possible. Spelling and punctuation corrections have been kept to a minimum in the entries quoted directly in these pages to help preserve their original character, spirit and intent.

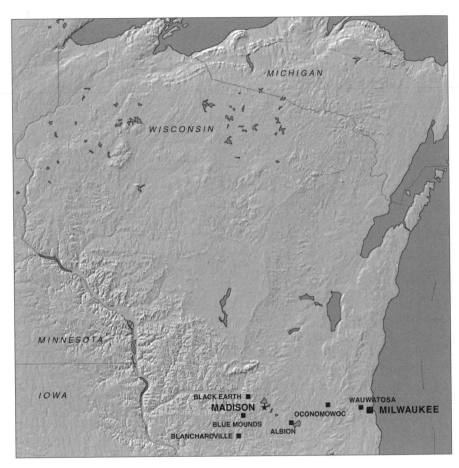

Alva, Alex & Clara's Wisconsin. (Relief map courtesy of Ray Sterner, Johns Hopkins University)

Chapter One

BLACK EARTH

*A*lva Adams hardly is an unknown character in western history. His accomplishments included election to the first Colorado State Legislature in 1876, success as a businessman, and later, becoming governor of Colorado. He also erected the first building on the Colorado Springs townsite, completing it on August 7, 1871.[4]

Adams was head of a Colorado political dynasty. A partial listing of his family namesakes includes not only Adams City and Adams County, but also the Alva B. Adams Tunnel, which brings water across the Continental Divide from Grand Lake to the Big Thompson River in Estes Park and is named for his son, a former U.S. senator. In addition, Adams State College was named after Alva's brother, long-time San Luis Valley resident William "Billy" Adams, who became a state senator and governor of Colorado. Another brother, Frank Adams, who had managed a store in Black Earth, Wisconsin, before moving to Colorado, became a political boss in Denver and all of Colorado, and was, for a time, apparently more powerful than his two brothers were during their gubernatorial terms, according to a Madison, Wisconsin, newspaper.[5]

For all of Alva Adams' later fame, little has been written about his formative years. It is often forgotten that when he relocated to the embryonic Colorado Springs, he was a lonely lad a thousand miles away from anything he knew, in a place that was home to little more than rocks and rolling grasslands. Just 21 years old and running a lumber business, he was not the lawyer he had intended to be. Nor was he the image of the governor he would become.

Like most of the players in Colorado's early history, Adams was born elsewhere, in south-central Wisconsin in 1850. His pioneering spirit and leadership skills likely were instilled by his parents. His mother, Eliza Blanchard Adams, was a native of New York State and the sister of Alvin Blanchard, founder of the village of Blanchardville, Wisconsin. His father, John Adams, hailed from Kentucky. When John was about 20 years old, he moved to Wisconsin to work in the lead mines. He then became a farmer, a country storekeeper and later, a produce dealer and livestock buyer.

After the Adams family moved to Black Earth, Wisconsin, in 1863, John Adams became sheriff of Dane County. In time, he was thrice elected to the state legislature, serving with some distinction.[6] This proved distracting for young Alva, who found politics and the state house in Madison much more interesting than the college-preparatory school at the University of Wisconsin where he was enrolled.

In the 1870 census, John Adams' real estate holdings were valued at $10,000 and his personal property at $15,000. After 1875, he gave up his store and devoted himself to buying and selling farms, becoming the largest holder of real estate in Dane and Iowa counties in Wisconsin. He also owned several farms in neighboring Iowa.[7]

In addition to his many achievements, the name chosen for the village where he had earlier built a grist mill and opened the first store was Adamsville. John Adams clearly was a man to be reckoned with.

Alva's older brother, Charles, was born in Pokerville, Wisconsin, also known as West Blue Mounds. It's now a ghost town. Brothers Alva, George, John and Frank were born in a log cabin somewhere near John Adams' store at a flourishing mining center and stagecoach station near Blue Mounds. Their younger sister, Elizabeth (Libbie), was born at Adamsville.

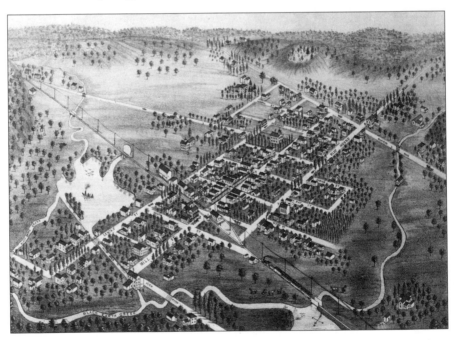

This lithograph offers a birds-eye view of Black Earth, a small town that raised people with big ambitions. (State Historical Society of Wisconsin)

Brothers William and Henry were born at West Blue Mounds and Clarence at Black Earth.

Alva's boyhood home, Black Earth was an important trading center in the 1860s and 1870s. It had grain elevators and a department store, and local businesses hauled and sold all the wood used by the wood-burning locomotives of the Chicago, Milwaukee & St. Paul Railroad. Black Earth was the market center for the Blue Mounds country, and an important stagecoach depot. Men and women from Black Earth made their mark in life.

Alva Adams described his childhood days in Black Earth: "Father provided well for his family, but it was Mother who was always caring for us all and guiding us. She had the home virtues. Father was the business partner." Alva also asserted that although he was born in a log cabin, he was never hungry, poor or over-worked. His memories were happy ones:

There were no rich, nor were there any in want. It was a genuine democracy. There was no caste. Hired man and girl ate with the family and guests, if there were any. We came from field or barn, and a wash at the pump was our preparation for table or bed. Food and clothing were plenty if not fashionable, and as all were alike there was no rivalry. . . . If poor we did not know it. That, in the true analysis, is riches.

Responsibilities were put on boys. At ten, each boy in our family owned a horse. They were ours to use, care for and sell. The boy's colt was never father's horse. We were encouraged to trade as a means of developing our business instinct.

By present standards, how poor we were. Compared to the means of our neighbors we were near affluence.

The main difference between the Adams family and their neighbors, if there was any, was that they were rather better off; that they did have books and magazines and papers, and that there was a closer community of interest between parents and children than is usual.[8]

In 1863, when Alva had just turned 13, he left home and offered his services to the Union side in the Civil War. Boys were supposed to be 18 to enlist, but at 15 they were eligible to become drummer boys. The feeling that "the boy who could not tell a lie in defense of his country is no red-blooded American" ran strong, but Alva, a frail boy who may have looked 13 and not a day older, was not accepted, even as a drummer boy.

Young Adams' unsuccessful attempt to enlist occurred the same year he began school at Albion Academy. It is unknown whether Alva received a degree from the school upon his scheduled graduation date in 1870. The academy's records are incomplete due to a disastrous fire which consumed the main building in 1915 and another blaze which destroyed the school's museum in 1965, five years after it opened.[9] There is evidence that Adams may have received his degree after he went west, perhaps on one of the several occasions when he returned to his old school to deliver an address. However, a letter his mother, Eliza Adams, wrote her friend, Mary Barnes McNatt, implies that Alva graduated with his class.[10]

In spite of the Wisconsin Constitution's provision in 1848 – the year Wisconsin became a state – that anyone between the ages of 4 and 20 should receive free schooling, only two thirds of all eligible youngsters were enrolled a decade later. Those who attended went to school scarcely more than 5 1/2 months each year. Public support for education in Wisconsin at the elementary level had been more enthusiastic than it was for secondary education. Public high schools had not yet been considered, but the Wisconsin's State Legislature chartered about 50 private academies to serve as college-preparatory schools during the mid-19th century.[11]

It was not until 1875 that the Wisconsin law providing for free high schools finally was enforced. Alva Adams' parents, however, already were at work providing their children with an education. In addition to furnishing their youngsters with books, magazines and newspapers, they enrolled Alva in nearby Albion Academy, presumably planning to send him to college sometime afterward.[12]

Although it has been claimed that Alva acquired an education typical among country boys in Wisconsin – Adams referred to it as "common school,"[13] – both Alva and his childhood sweetheart, Clara Heeney, were able to get a better-than-average education in that state. The Adams and Heeney families could afford private secondary and college-preparatory schooling for their children, and they willingly provided it.

Records indicate Alva transferred to the college-preparatory school at the University of Wisconsin during the 1868-1869 school year with the expectation of graduating in 1872. But he never received his diploma. Colorado would be his new home that year.

Clara's story provides additional insights into education on the frontier, as well as illustrating some of the difficulties encountered by young women, the place of women in early education and the arts, and what it was like to attend or teach at frontier schools.

When the Adams family moved to Black Earth, Alva was 13 and Clara was 11. The two became well acquainted, not only at school but also at church and Sunday school. Clara and Alva shared a deep affection for each other, and she saved the letters he wrote her throughout her life.

(Top) This frame house in Black Earth was home to the Heeney and Burton families. (State Historical Society of Wisconsin)... (Bottom) Clara (center) patiently posed with her mother, Georgianna, and sister, Amanda, when this photograph was taken in the mid-1800s. (MacGregor Ranch)

The first letter from Alva preserved among Clara's personal possessions was received in early December, 1866, when she was 14 years old. Adams mentioned in the letter that he might not see her for three months as he would be going back to Albion Academy in a little over a week. When he had missed her at Sunday school and church, Adams went to the Heeney house to see her, but was told by her sister, Amanda, that she had already gone back to Madison, where she was enrolled at the University of Wisconsin's Normal Preparatory College.

Clara was 13 when her father, Thomas Heeney, died on October 25,

This student's desk was used at Albion Academy. A sign outside the school's lone remaining building states, "Albion Academy graduated many outstanding students, including Alva Adams, governor of Colorado." Adams may not have formally completed his studies at Albion. (Albion Academy Historical Museum)

1865, at age 49, leaving his widow, Georgianna, and two daughters, Clara and Amanda, 16. Amanda was 17 the next year when she married Carlos Burton, a farmer, in August of 1866. Carlos and Amanda made their home with Clara and Georgianna in Black Earth.

That same year, at age 14, Clara became one of the first females enrolled at the fledgling preparatory school for girls at the state university in Madison. Opened to women only three years earlier, the Normal Preparatory College offered what was essentially a high school course of instruction.

We may never know why Georgianna and Clara decided that the young girl should attend the preparatory school for young ladies rather than Albion Academy. Perhaps Clara did not wish to recite in the same classrooms with male students, which was permitted at the academy. Perhaps the art classes offered by the university helped her make the choice. It is quite possible that her mother was convinced it would be best if Clara did not attend the same boarding school as her young sweetheart, Alva Adams.

Albion Academy opened its doors to both men and women on an equal footing upon its establishment in 1854, making it the first coeducational institution in the state. At the University of Wisconsin, it was an entirely different matter. Females were accepted at the Normal Preparatory College, but they were not admitted to the University of Wisconsin until the Civil War depleted male enrollment.

At age 15, Clara was among the first young women admitted to the university's newly established Female College, entering after she completed a year of preparatory school. She was accepted in 1867 as a member of the Junior Class. Clara was listed as a member of the Senior Class in 1869-1870, but she did not graduate.[14] The *Catalogue of the Officers and Students of the University of Wisconsin 1868-1869, Female College* explained that young ladies who did not desire to graduate might "enter at any time, and pursue any study of the term for which they might be prepared."

Paul A. Chadbourne, president of the University of Wisconsin from 1866 until 1870, the same years Clara was a student in Madison, strictly forbade the admission of women. But the Civil War forced him to back down on his decree. In 1867, he was compelled to admit females, but he insisted upon separate classes for the men and women.[15] Not until 1874, four years after Clara was a student in Madison, were women finally admitted to the university's regular student body.

Despite the university's segregation of the sexes, Clara apparently received her share of male attention. In her earliest preserved diary, written mostly in 1870 when she was 17 to 18 years old, her March 15, 1870, entry divulged that after being serenaded, she had the audacity to throw a bouquet of flowers out the window, angering her teachers.

That spring, Clara left the University of Wisconsin. The Black Earth census of July 26, 1870, listed Clara Heeney as 18 years old and a schoolteacher. In the summer of 1870, she taught at a "three-month school," probably in or near Stoner's Prairie, Township of Fitchburg, Dane County, Wisconsin. There were 10 schools in this township, two located close to the property of the family of Clara Stevens, Clara Heeney's friend and classmate.

Clara's Milwaukee Female College days were often unhappy as the youthful woman pondered her future. (Milwaukee County Historical Society)

In her diary, Clara recorded the beginning of her brief "common-school" teaching career:

Saturday, April 30 – Today I came to Stoner's Prairie, called at Dr. Hayes'. Mr. Stevens and Clara (her friend and classmate) met me there, rode out to their house from Madison in a carriage. Had my hair shingled.

Sunday, May 1 – We did not go to church. I feel very tired.

Monday, May 2 – Today my school of three months begins. I am afraid I will not like the school, but will try to do my duty. I see the school has been poorly governed and the teachers have not been good ones. I will have my hands full to train them.

At that time, students were instructed in the subjects of reading, spelling, writing, geography, mental arithmetic, written arithmetic, English grammar and history, a demanding load for both the teachers and their students.

After completing her May-through-July, 1870, teaching assignment, Clara was not satisfied with her role. She decided to further her education. She entered Milwaukee Female College in September, 1870, enrolling in courses oriented toward the arts.

Clara's diary offers glimpses of her college days – her interests, her worries and her mixed emotions. She copied recipes and remedies, told of teas and parties, and mentioned pretty dresses she was sewing. There were activities at church and school and meetings of the Castalian Society, a group organized by the ladies of the college.

In her diary entry on September 29, 1870, Clara mentioned the nice-looking conductor on the street car. She also praised the fine-art exhibit at the State Fair in Milwaukee and referred to Olivet Congregational Church, the Dutch Market and the Whittemore Book Store. On October 24, she noted that she wore her gymnastics suit for the first time. The November 30 *Black Earth Advertiser* offered contrasting views of exercise for women, stating its personal preference for domestic pursuits:

Housework for Girls: It is the law of God that no human being can have a sound, vigorous body, accomplish much physically, and enjoy a long life without good muscles. Though there is a variety of ways by which exercise may be obtained, yet domestic labor is best adapted to develop and strengthen the whole system. . . . No kind of work for girls is so calculated as household work to develop all the muscles of the body – to do it in early life, and gradually under circumstances is favorable to health generally. The girls and woman must thus be trained year after year, otherwise she will never obtain that hardihood of constitution, that strength of muscle, that power of endurance; or, in other words, that balance of temperament so essential to good health and happiness in all the social and domestic regulations of life.

In her diary, Clara noted that she convinced one of her classmates to go with her to see if they might visit her friend, Ida Bean of Madison, who was enrolled at St. Mary's Institute, a religious boarding school near Milwaukee Female College operated by the Sisters of Notre Dame. On October 6, they

"Such walls, they cast such a shadow." This impressive complex is Milwaukee's St. Mary's Institute. (Sisters of Notre Dame)

walked up to the "nunnery," as Clara termed it. The acquaintance they called on pleaded a headache, and they did not get to see her. Clara's diary entry made her feelings quite clear about the place: "Such walls, they cast such a shadow. How can those nuns shut themselves up so?"

Information provided by the Motherhouse of the School Sisters of Notre Dame, Milwaukee, saw things differently:

This Institute, founded in 1850, is situated in one of the most elevated and healthy locations of Milwaukee, and commands an extensive view of the city and its environs while pleasure grounds adjoining the building afford ample advantage for healthful exercise.

The system of education under the direction of the School Sisters of Notre Dame embraced every useful and ornamental branch suitable for young ladies: languages, needlework, music, drawing, painting and religious instruction.

Clara ran the emotional gamut during her time in Milwaukee. The study of art, landscape painting in particular, became her passion. She was especially happy to finish her painting of "Trenton Falls. . . . quite pretty." But the very next day, she was depressed. "I am home again. My health will not permit me to go to school longer." Her entry that day concluded with, "Will they give me some peace?"

It is not known whether her anguish was caused by beaus, teachers or some other problem. It is uncertain whether her fatigue or illness had physical or emotional causes. Clara admitted that she feared one instructor in particular, an outstanding teacher but one who was under much pressure to make the school a financial success. Clara confided in her diary, "I wish I was not so afraid of Miss Mortimer. I try so hard to please her and she seems so cross with me."[16] It is also possible that Clara may have experienced some discomforts of arthritis. Years later, the 1880 Census for Estes Park[17] listed her as being infirm with rheumatism. Her mother is known to have suffered from rheumatism in 1875.

Clara's diary claimed she did return to the college, however, and a memorandum added at the back of her 1870 entries concluded that the year had been one of the saddest of her life, "with many ups and downs in the beginning." But Clara was a determined young woman, writing, "I am quite discouraged, but I see improvement, with faith and perseverance I hope to conquer." Clara may have been unhappy early in the year because of her prospects of teaching school when she most wanted to study landscape painting. This would partially explain her June 6, 1870, entry: "I am so tired but I dont want to go to B.E. Oh would that I could go somewhere else."

It wouldn't take long for Clara to become truly convinced that art was her calling. The following September, she earned honors in the fine-arts competition at the third annual Fair of the Wisconsin Valley Agricultural Society in Black Earth for her oil painting landscapes.

The fair proved a family affair. Clara's mother, Georgianna Heeney, won first premium for her chromolithograph; five first premiums in the "fruits and flowers" category, including "monthly rose" and "sweet scented geranium, pelargonium;" and 16 assorted first and second premiums for her pickled fruits, preserves and jellies. Clara's sister, Amanda, and Libbie (Elizabeth) Adams, Alva's only sister, both were cited in the category of "domestic manufactures, ornamental and fancy needle work." Amanda's husband, Carlos Burton, won prizes for his Suffolk boar and Norway oats.

John Adams won first premium for his span of carriage horses and his suckling colt. John Adams and Georgianna Heeney served as judges at the fair. The Adams and Heeney families continued to be closely acquainted in Black Earth, which may have brought Clara and Alva closer together.

A year after Clara's three-month schoolteaching assignment, Alva reminisced in a letter remembering the days in Black Earth when as young teenagers, they were sweethearts at "winter school." Her short diary of 1870-1871 had only one surprisingly uninteresting and non-committal entry concerning Alva, that of May 7, 1870: "Today my friend is twenty in a short time."

The pages torn from her diary might have furnished other clues about their friendship. It is possible that some of her unhappiness that spring was due to a small falling-out with Alva. She may also have been worried about Alva's health or fretted over the possibility that they might be separated further.

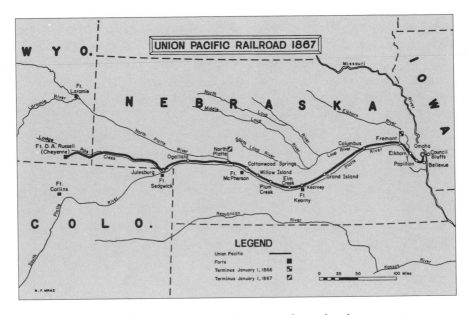

The Adams party followed much of the Union Pacific Railroad route on its course through the vast expanse of Nebraska. (Union Pacific Historical Museum)

Chapter Two

A TRIP OF DESPERATION

During the winter of 1870-1871, concerns over their children's health compelled John and Eliza Adams to begin making plans to move to Colorado.

All of the children were quite susceptible to respiratory illness. It is likely that the boys suffered from tuberculosis, which they may have developed while working in their father's warehouses. Although the July 30, 1870, Black Earth Census showed that Alva was "Attending University," young Adams remained at home that fall because of his illness. With hopes of maintaining the family's Wisconsin roots and someday even returning, his mother, Eliza, wrote her friend, Mary McNatt, "We talk of going to Colorado. I shall go. Mr. Adams will remain here to close his businesses. It seems dreadful to think of leaving. . . ."

An unsettled feeling must have prevailed at the Adams home shortly before the decision to head west. The death of Alva's older brother, Charles, in June of 1870 could have compelled the change in Alva's plans to go to college. The family's feeling of urgency also may have been precipitated by

This is an uncovered Studebaker. (Art courtesy of Elyse Deffke Bliss)

the earlier deaths of 2-year-old Henry in 1865 and baby Clarence in 1869. To compound the family's worries, neither George nor Alva was well. According to one recollection:

Charles (had failed) almost day by day; Alva was very frail; George looked as if he might sink into a decline at any day. With the courage and hope that characterizes tuberculosis, none of the boys was willing to admit that he was ill. The disease had been acquired working in their father's dusty warehouse, and in those days when the windows were nailed down and heavy paper pasted around the frames, fresh air was regarded as our worst enemy instead of our best friend. Winter was the signal for excluding every breath from the outer world. Straw or papers were put under the carpets and sweeping day distributed germs freshly. Added to these conditions a hearty and "unbalanced" diet and the wonder is that so many survived rather than that so few perished.[18]

The Adams decided to take their doctor's advice and emigrate to the Rocky Mountains. The *Black Earth Advertiser* reported that the John Adams family left Black Earth for Colorado on May 8, 1871. The Adams were to travel by wagon as their doctor advised them against making the trip by train because he felt rail travel was too quick and could be dangerous for patients with lung ailments. According to the newspaper's account:

They had been busy making preparations for their journey for some weeks, and were delayed due to bad weather the last week. Their destination is Denver, where they plan to remain until next winter. Should the climate not agree with them, their plan is to move on as far as New Mexico.

The trip is solely to benefit the health of the Adams children, and no pains or expense were spared to provide every possible convenience. The Adams family will take three new wagons, one of which is a spring wagon. Of their eight horses, seven are large draught horses and the other a good riding horse. Alva, in charge of the expedition, will make a first-rate "captain" of the party, consisting of Mrs. Adams, five younger children and two hired men. Accompanying the party as far as Blanchardville, Mr. Adams indicates that he desires to dispose of his entire property here and then go south to remain with his family.

Two of the wagons were manufactured by Myres and Voss of this village. Made especially for this trip to be taken by the Adams' family, the wagons are of the very best manufacture and finished up in tip top style.

Alva was 21 years old in 1871, when he left his Wisconsin home and his sweetheart, Clara. At that young age, he was entrusted with leading the expedition to Colorado, and with bringing his mother and the five younger children safely to the new frontier by covered wagon.

Alva began recording their journey on May 8, 1871, in Blanchardville. In his journal, Adams referred to the trip's "indefinite destination, but somewhere in the region of the Rocky Mountains. Object – direct – health – indirect and incidental – support and profit."[19] On May 10, the journey was delayed as the family was detained by a defective wagon and a sick horse. The Adams had to barter for a new horse and go to Monroe to procure a new wagon.

During the journey, Alva faithfully recorded his travels in his journal, kept up his correspondence with Clara and wrote columns for the *Black Earth Advertiser* under the assumed name of Dane. Alva's travel letters and stories for the *Advertiser* conveyed a strong sense of his personality. These articles portrayed his opinions better than any of his other writings. They stood in marked contrast to the lonely letters that Alva sent to Clara during this period.

There is no record of letters from Alva to Clara from the time she was 14 until five years later on her 19th birthday, May 9, 1871. However, their paths crossed many times, both in Madison and in Black Earth, during those years. During 1868 and 1869, both were in Madison at the University of Wisconsin, Alva at the Preparatory College and Clara at the Female College. When Alva wrote to her on her 19th birthday, he was departing for the West. This letter gave no indication as to Clara's whereabouts at the time. Her diary and autograph album suggested that she was still at Milwaukee Female College and had not yet gone to Chicago to attend classes at that city's Academy of Design. However, Alva's letter furnished the important clue that Clara was determined not to marry until she was 21.

Young Alva penned the birthday greetings as he left on the family's prairie schooner journey to Colorado. His letter to Clara was written on stationery bearing a "B" monogram, presumably at the home of Adams' grandmother, Elizabeth Brown Blanchard, in Blanchardville.

The bottom of the page was torn off. Perhaps Clara did not want anyone else to read this missing portion. Maybe she was unhappy over something Alva had written. But she continued to save his letters, including this one:

Blanchardville
May 9, 1871

   Sweet Nineteen,

   Two years from today, it seems a long time to wait yet I know not that it may be for the best for with me a part, if not all of that time, is not my own and must be devoted to the task that has been assigned to me — that task may be a detriment or a benefit — a prelude to a life's failure or a key to prosperity — it may be an obsticle to my success or it may be but the purifying fire that will prepare me to more successfully work out the problems of life.

But be it what it may, an obsticle or an incentive, it is a duty that must be performed and one — no matter how contrary to my desires — which I will endeavor to perform to the utmost.

Have thought considerable of the determination you have made and have concluded that it must be founded upon good grounds and in consequence I will not again broach the subject until the limitation expires. If til then you stand the test and remain the same as now, you will be worthy the Life effort of any man even Paul, Johnnie or — "The fellow that looks like me."

Actually have not the time today to write a letter but could not resist the temptation to write as it may be the aniversary of a day of importance to me.

Shall not on the above grounds ask to be excused for brevity for I have no great incentive to write a long letter as we are not decided.

From June 1871, to March 1872, the *Black Earth Advertiser* published the letters of a traveler named Dane who was headed from Black Earth to Dubuque and Omaha through Nebraska's Platte Valley to Fort Kearny, Wyoming Territory, and on to Julesburg, Greeley, Denver, Colorado City, Pikes Peak and Colorado Springs.

The June 8 *Advertiser* mentioned that private letters from John Adams' family indicated the party had reached Omaha, and that all were enjoying improved health. The first letter to the *Advertiser* from Alva published under the Dane nom de plume was merely signed "Omaha:"

The Advertiser, June 15, 1871
Overland Correspondence, Omaha, NB
June 1st, 1871
The life of an emigrant is a life of many vicissitudes, of mingled good and bad, of the agreeable and the unpleasant, of the grotesque and the serious; but to the true traveler and observer it is replete with engaging interest. The changing scenes, the shifting panorama ever excites and retains his attention and dispels the monotony. It is not to him the plodding journey alone, a pilgrimage to Mecca, a disagreeable means to a desired end; but it is likewise a voyage of discovery and observation. Nowhere is this more evident than in a journey along the old emigrant trail from Dubuque to Omaha. The first few miles west of the metropolis of Iowa

does not present a very inviting aspect, it being over those bluffy hills which characterizes the banks of the Northern Mississippi. But anon the prospects brighten, broad and rolling prairies greet the eye. On either side lie the fertile fields, rich in the growing grain, and giving brilliant promises of an abundant harvest.

Our journey progresses, the same scenes continue, the same rolling prairie, the same fertile land; the broad expanse ever relieved by the many belts of timber that jem the banks of the numerous streams and rivers. Many towns are passed through; all giving evidence of the thrift, energy and enterprise of their inhabitants, and conclusive testimony of the prosperity and wealth of the tributary country, excepting a few supperannuated villages born under the auspices of a few deluded speculators who were imbued with the ideas of their soon becoming railroad and commercial centers; but alas, for human hopes! The roads were built but passed through some rival town, leaving them totally eclipsed in their infancy, a monument of glories departed — of prosperity anticipated but never realized.

As we approach the center of the State, a scarcity of timber manifests itself in the miles of wire fences that here enclose many of the fields, contemperaneous with this deficiency of timber and fuel, we enter the limits of the coal regions, inexhaustible beds of which article underlies a large part of the State of Iowa; thus affording a strong illustration of the economy and wise provisions of nature in supplying the actual necessities of a territory with an ample substitute.

Emmigration appears to have received a new impulse this spring, and Iowa people stand aghast at the innumerable trains of "desert ships" that are wending their way through their State for the anticipated elderrado beyond. The majority of these wanderers, they maintain, come from Wisconsin, and they begin to think that State rapidly depopulating. Regarding it as Douglas did Vermont, "A good State to emigrate from." They know not that when one departs, others come, that another arm drives the plow that has been resigned by its former dissatisfied proprietor, that other and more earnest hands assume the duties neglected by their vacillating and unstable fellows.

As a Kansas newspaper noted, "Following the close of the Civil War, the tempo of the westward migration was greatly accelerated. During the conflict, the far West had increased rapidly in population and even the immediate trans-Mississippi West had felt increasing growing pains. But border troubles, the threat of Indians and the lack of rapid methods of transportation retarded large population shifts to the Great Plains West."

Cessation of Civil War hostilities and the impetus given by the Homestead Act of 1862 – accompanied by renewed interest and effort in building railroads westward beyond the Missouri River – brought a flood of immigrants to the plains. It was, according to the Lawrence, Kansas, newspaper, "the most astonishing migratory movement which has characterized any age or nation." [20]

Tradition has preserved the idea that gold alone lured newcomers to the territories west of the Mississippi, but health, as well as wealth, was important to early settlers. . . . .[21] In the 19th century, many physicians recommended Colorado and the Rockies as cures for tuberculosis-prone patients. In pre-vaccine days, the only apparent treatments for the disease were rest and fresh air at mountain resorts.

Besides health, in the words of one author, "the reasons for heading to the 'lands beyond sundown' were as varied as the men and women the West attracted. Sheer adventure drew some; the promise of fertile land or hope for religious freedom impelled others. Very often, the motive was gold fever or expectation of profitable trade – what Ralph Waldo Emerson termed 'a very commonplace wish to find a short way to wealth.'" [22] Many others came to see the Rocky Mountains and decided to make their homes in the area.

Pure adventure also was a potent lure. Said writer Richard M. Ketchum of the western exodus:

There was something that literally drove men westward, goading them across the endless mountains, through steep passes, across searing plains and desert, into the face of terrors known and those unguessed. It was vision, it was courage, it was at times the sheer joy of overcoming fantastic obstacles. And it was also the conviction that what they were doing was different from anything that had happened before, that nothing would ever be quite the same again, and that the world would be a better place for what they had accomplished.[23]

In addition to the reports of the Adams family's trip west as written by Alva to Clara and by Alva as Dane, the anonymous and very mature overland correspondent for the *Advertiser*, Adams' only sister, Libbie, 12 years old at the time of the journey, later offered her own recollections of the trip:

There were three wagons, all of them Studebakers. Two carried baggage and Father had the other built like an army ambulance. Alva drove one and two men who had worked for Father for a long time and so were well known to us all drove the others.

We had extra horses beside the three span – two to relieve the teams if anything happened, and two ponies, one for Billy (little brother, age 10,

18

*also called Willie, who was destined to become both a state senator and
governor of Colorado) and one for me to ride, but we sold one of the ponies
when we were crossing Iowa. A man took a fancy to him and followed along
a whole day, until he finally got the pony. We knew that when we got past
Council Bluffs it wouldn't do for us to ride because we might get away from
the wagon and there were rumors of Indian troubles. We did not go with the
other wagon trains however, because we could go much faster alone.*[24]

*Westward wagon travel was a slow, plodding and sometimes dangerous proposition.
(Greeley Museums)*

The Adams family made the decision to follow the Union Pacific
Railroad course on the journey west. The expedition's leader, Alva, was a
very observant individual, making him a capable correspondent for the
Advertiser. As Dane, he reported to his readers from Wyoming Territory on
June 30 that the stations along the railway were usually insignificant, the
majority consisting of a depot and a section house. If a station was larger,
Adams wrote, it surely dispensed that spirit so much a part of western lore:

*Where there are more than this, the third house is the inevitable grocery
and liquor vending establishment. Whisky! The mystery of the age; the curse
of the United States; ever the first article of commerce on the borders of civilization; the constant companion of those brave and hardy pioneers who first
subdue and conquer the wilderness. Is it an agent of or an enemy to the
advancement of civilization? Many here maintain that it is a stimulus that
enables man to better endure the hardships of pioneer life and that without
its influence, man would more often be defeated in the great contest between
nature, the savage and civilized energy. We discuss the question neither pro
or con, merely giving it as a matter of fact pertaining to western life, leaving*

*it with the reader to determine in his own mind whether the forces of nature
could not be more easily subdued, the wily savage more easily overcome.
Whether a higher standard of manhood would not be established, a higher
degree of moral excellence attained without than with this agent, whether it is
not an influence more potent for evil than good.*

Alva Adams was an aggressive temperance man. One newspaper later
called attention to the "fearsome fact that when the delegates who had
nominated Adams (for governor) marched down the street and filed into a
saloon, he utterly refused to accompany them. He not only would not
drink, but he would not stand by and see others drink."[25]

Adams also was a man sensitive enough to see the human components
that comprised the great westward tide of humanity. One of his most
poignant Dane columns for the *Advertiser* during the long trip through the
Platte Valley expressed his sentiments clearly:

*Many an unknown grave is seen, nameless and many without a mark.
One we saw burdened with the fragrant flowers and the wild roses of the
prairie, the last tribute of a loving hand to the loved one who lies here
entombed upon the boundless prairie, beneath the vigils of the silent stars.
What life histories are contained in these lonely graves – of boyant hopes
here buried – of ambition wrecked. They are eloquent of suffering and
anguish, of the strong hearts whose life lamps were here extinguished in
the dreary wilderness, away from civilization, friends, home, with no fond
hand to cool the fevered brow, with no loving voice to soothe the dying
hour, alone and friendless, the last spark expired. A grassy mound is all
that remains of the father, husband or brother, whose loved ones will watch
for the return of him who will return no more forever. These are relics of
the great human stampede of 1859, when like a simoom the myriads of
the east swept through the valley enrout for the Alladins garden of the
Rocky Mountains. What a sight was this: the silent valley which for untold
ages had remained undisturbed in its original wildness suddenly trans-
formed into an avenue of life, bustle and activity. The adjoining hills
returned the echo of a thousand voices, the astonished skies looked down
upon a thousand campfires.*

Alva continued his report to his hometown newspaper with disturbing
news of "depredatious and hostile raids" by Indians. He criticized the government's policies as inefficient and blamed its pardoning tendencies for
many of the outrages committed: "To be compelled to make a traveling arse-
nal of himself; to unite with the symbols of peace the implements of war; to
feel each night that ere the morning dawns, his entire stock may be driven

off, his house destroyed and himself and family the victims of barbarities. This is the ordeal that will convert any man from the strongest humanitarianism to the most rabid exterminationist. The result is as certain as the effect produced by the contact of fire and wood, of heat and snow."

While these opinions regarding the Indian situation seem unbelievably harsh today, they were not unusual in 1871. The esteemed editor of the *Rocky Mountain News*, William N. Byers, on February 15, 1871, suggesting in print that rather than wasting dollars promoting the explorations of Major John Wesley Powell in the Colorado River Canyon, the government should have spent its money "killing Apaches." Byers later changed his mind about the importance of Powell's expedition.

Libbie Adams, some years after the journey to Colorado, recalled that the wagon trains directly preceding and following the Adams party had been attacked by Indians. This is highly unlikely, although it is possible that these were the kinds of rumors the emigrants heard. Noted one historical account, "Encounters with hostile Indians – often much embellished – are far more conspicuous in latter-day reminiscent accounts than in the journals and diaries in which overland emigrants recorded the actual events of their journey." Both overlanders and guidebook writers agreed that thievery, not murderous attack, was the major threat posed by Indians.[26]

Libbie explained that when they reached Fort Kearny, the soldiers were determined they should not go on. The military men told them it was a dreadful thing for a woman and children to take such a risk. "Of course none of us realized what a chance we were taking, but our men thought they knew better than the soldiers," Libbie remembered. But the great promise of the land to the west proved too hard to resist, and the Adams expedition pushed on.

Not only did the Adams men think they knew better than the Fort Kearny soldiers, but they also apparently thought they knew better than any woman, as illustrated by Alva's first reactions to the changing times. When the Adams' wagons reached Wyoming, "Overland Correspondent" Alva in his July 17, 1871, column painfully expressed his astonishment and disillusionment over meeting a woman voter. His attitude reflected what was widespread in those days: Women's suffrage in the United States was considered by males to be no more than a subject for humorous remarks or bitter condemnation. According to one recollection, "Miners discussed it around their camp fires, and freighters on their long, slow journeys over the mountain trails argued pro and con whether they should 'let' women have the ballot."[27]

Adams' July 17, Dane column related:

We passed through the southeastern corner of Wyoming. . . . an immense bed of small gravel, and if the portion traversed is a true specimen and criterion of the entire territory, its agricultural prospects are far from encouraging. But Wyoming, if great in nothing, has, at last, achieved notoriety by being the first to admit women into the political kingdom. Here it was that we first beheld that political monstrosity, a female voter. She appeared like unto other women. Her baby was just as neat apparently, without any forebodings of the future, and she was just as willing to praise and hear extolled his beauties as other mothers, still, under the yoke, she did not wear pantaloons, neither did she smoke nor invite us to partake of a social glass, there to discuss the political problems of the day. She had voted at the last election, but "really she had forgotten for whom, but supposed it made no difference." Home was evidently her sphere. Politics she eschewed, and when the subject was introduced, became suddenly listless and uninterested. Talk of babies, domestic and material duties and her interest was excited, she became eloquent and interesting. Ever true to the instincts of the mother and the wife. Womanly but not manly. Than this no higher praise can be sung of woman, no brighter crown be placed on woman's brow.

Women of the 19th century were expected to be diligent wives, mothers and housekeepers. The home was regarded as the proper "place" for women in society. For the wealthy woman, this meant a life of leisure. For others, it forecast the endless drudgery of housework and homemaking. Without full legal standing or widespread educational opportunities, most women could not by themselves escape the domestic confines. But pioneer life leveled the playing field somewhat, according to author Joanna L. Stratton:

To the pioneer woman, home and hearth meant work loads that were heavier than ever. And yet that work was the work of survival. In its isolation, the pioneer family existed as a self-sufficient unit that took pride in its ability to provide for itself and persevere in the face of hardship. Men and women worked together as partners, combining their strengths and talents to provide food and clothing for themselves and their children. As a result, women found themselves on a far more equal footing with their spouses.[28]

A short time after Alva had encountered the "woman who voted," his family camped at Greeley. Adams and his mother went to hear women's rights advocates Susan B. Anthony and Elizabeth Cady Stanton speak. After listening to their orations and reading the feminist free love paper distributed by Stanton at the close of the lecture, Alva was furious. As the anonymous Dane, in his July 17, 1871, column he told the *Advertiser's* readers:

Colorado appears to be the vineyard wherein the female suffragists are laboring assidiously, probably expecting to reap the harvest of another territory victimized into committing itself to their cause. Their "cannons," Anthony and Stanton, have been of late canvassing the territory. At Greeley we heard Mrs. Stanton deliver her oration. She indulged in the customary pathos when speaking of the galling serfdom of women and how they are tyranized over by the monster, man. She enlarged considerably upon their new discovery — that under the fourteenth and fifteenth amendments a declaratory act from Congress asserting their citizenship is all that is necessary to entitle them to the ballot. At the close of the lecture she distributed Woodhull and Claflins free love paper. Thus tacitly avowing and symbolizing the unity of the two causes.

Dane

Through their publication *Woodhull & Claflin's Weekly,* sisters Victoria (Claflin) Woodhull and Tennessee "Tennie" C. Claflin attempted to influence the women's rights movement with articles proposing free love, short skirts, easier divorce laws, world government, public housing, magnetic healing, birth control, abortion and legalized prostitution. The seductive sisters, whose past activities allegedly had included healing scams, blackmail and prostitution, also managed to convince aging financier Cornelius Vanderbilt to back them in a stock brokerage enterprise that would prove quite profitable, ranking the pair among the most alluring brokers that ever operated.[29]

Libbie was not taken along to hear the suffragists speak, and later recalled no comments from her mother or her brother about the occasion. However, "Mother always regretted that she burned the journal in which she wrote every day. There were many little things that would have been interesting to the children," she later remembered.[30] One guess is that Eliza Adams burned her journal because she was shocked over her own comments regarding the feminists' remarks.

Although Alva's attitude toward women matured considerably over the next few years, Clara, now an art student in Chicago and a cosmopolitan young woman, must have been uncomfortable with Alva's non-feminist beliefs. Certainly, his jibe "if til then you stand the test and remain the same as now, you will be worthy the Life effort of any man, even Paul, Johnnie or – 'The fellow that looks like me'" included in his letter of May 9, 1871, indicates his desire that Clara remain pure, sweet and maybe even unable to form her own opinions. Clara and Alva perhaps were drifting apart.

Upon the Adams family's arrival in Greeley, Colorado, Alva was hired to haul railroad ties from the mountains south of Denver for the building of the Denver and Rio Grande Railway. Adams may have begun working for a C.W. Sanborn in Greeley shortly before Sanborn's lumber yard was moved to Colorado Springs, possibly agreeing to transfer to the new location and settle there. According to the July 26, 1871, *Greeley Tribune,* Sanborn sold his interest in the Colony Lumber Yard on July 17. The *Tribune* on July 19 ran a news item mentioning that Sanborn had shipped to Pikes Peak 30,000 feet of lumber, 100 doors and 100 windows, along with a lot of moldings.

Clara was studying at Chicago's Academy of Design when it was destroyed in that city's great 1871 fire. (Chicago Public Library)

While delivering lumber to Colorado City, Alva arrived at the foot of Pikes Peak in time to observe an event that made history. On July 31, 1871, Adams watched the first stake being driven for the new townsite of Colorado Springs, marking the southeast corner of what is now Pikes Peak and Cascade avenues.

Commemorating the 50th anniversary of the driving of that first stake, Alva Adams remarked in his speech, "Fifty years ago today, sitting upon a load of lumber I witnessed the planting of the stake that marked the site of the coming city. A week later, as an employee of C.W. Sanborn, I completed and slept in the first house on site of Colorado Springs." [31]

Shortly after his arrival in his new hometown, Adams was hard at work. According to one published account:

While working for Mr. Sanborn, Mr. Adams set about building a struc-

ture that would answer for a lumber office, hardware store and dwelling place. By August he had completed a small building on South Cascade Avenue, which was the first building on the present site of Colorado Springs, and there the business was carried on. In October he bought the stock of goods from his employer, paying $4,100 therefor, and, as he did not have the cash in hand, he paid in notes bearing two per cent interest a month. Since then he has constantly, and with success, engaged in the hardware business.[32]

Concluding his column of July 31 for the *Black Earth Advertiser*, Adams as Dane described the brand-new town being developed at the foot of Pikes Peak. It was:

. . . .*a town as yet without a house, excepting the tented habitations of the invalid and tourist. A temporary hotel 140 by 23 feet, to be supplanted next spring by one of more imposing dimensions, is now in process of erection. Other improvements are contemplated, soon to be put into execution, designing the place as a favorite resort for the invalid and the pleasure seeker — the Saratoga of the West. Nor can we doubt but that these anticipations will be fully realized, for no place combines within so small a compass so many health giving properties, so many points of interest to*

Planners envisioned greatness for Colorado Springs, but Pikes Peak still overlooked a frontier town in the early 1870s. (Denver Public Library)

facinate and retain the traveler and the pleasure seeker. We need but cast our eyes a short distance into the future to behold this place a resort second to none. To see this valley and the surrounding hills blossoming with beautiful villas and lovely cottages, occupied not only by the lovers of rural life from our western towns and cities, but likewise by the inhabitants of the east who have come hither from the waning glories of eastern resorts to enjoy the mountain climate and behold the wonders of the West.

Dane

Alva's faith in the future of this new community founded under the name of the Fountain Colony of Colorado was not unwarranted. Newspapers on October 23, 1871, carried the story of the first regular passenger train service to Colorado Springs from Denver, inaugurated by the Denver and Rio Grande Railway. The trip took five hours each way at an average speed of 15 miles per hour.[33]

Colorado Springs was founded to support the railroad and offer a residential destination for settlers. The community served as a western resort

Railroad executive William Jackson Palmer founded Colorado Springs as a rail center and western resort. (Denver Public Library)

for visitors from the East and Europe. It also was seen as an excellent place to recover from the intractable diseases of the time. Riding at the point of the new development was General William J. Palmer, a noted Civil War Union Army cavalry leader and post-war railroad pioneer.

The founder of the Denver and Rio Grande Railway – and Colorado Springs itself – Palmer also envisioned the city becoming a utopian destination there in Pikes Peak country:

. . . .desiring to have a different sort of town, and to invite people of gentle breeding to come and make their homes here, notwithstanding the then remoteness and rather wild repute of this frontier, it was natural that we should desire to bring about conditions where the barroom with the gambling and dance halls should not be the chief human interest in evidence.[34]

A great attraction in the new community would be a resort destined to grow up around several mineral springs located in the shadow of 14,110-foot Pikes Peak. Palmer tried to give the 480-acre site surrounding the soda and iron springs a touch of elegance by calling it La Font or Villa La Font. But the name soon gave way to Manitou, the Algonquin Indian spirit or Great Spirit.

Pamphlet propaganda touting the Colorado Springs area's many natural and man-made amenities was so successful, particularly in England, that the new city soon was dubbed Little London. So rapidly did newcomers arrive

Manitou Springs quickly became a popular tourist stop. (Denver Public Library)

that a rush order was sent to Chicago for 150 portable houses to prevent suffering that first winter.[35]

For some years, the name Colorado Springs referred to a wide area, including the Garden of the Gods, Colorado City and the surrounding mineral springs. The new town of Colorado Springs quickly overshadowed Manitou Springs and Colorado City, and the name of the entire area officially became Colorado Springs when it was incorporated as part of Colorado Territory on September 2, 1872.

After Alva's arrival in Colorado Springs in late July, 1871, he wrote the following letter (excerpted here) to Clara, evidently in August. He used the letterhead of "C.W. Sanborn's Colony Yard, Eastern and Western Lumber, Timber." Alva crossed out "Greeley" on the stationery and wrote "Colorado Springs:"

Clara,

(Erased message, barely visible)

. . . . Since the receipt of your letter I have been thinking continualy, yet with no method to my thoughts, and have in consequence arrived at no satisfactory conclusion. Your letters always awaken a sensation of loneliness of something marking a void – which but one thing can fill and that event so far in the uncertain future that its realization seems fraught with doubt.

This office, the first completed building in this town, I have occupied for ten days entirely alone with the exception of business calls, Sanborn having gone to Denver for a short time leaving me in charge of his entire business. Have no companion, no society that is any way congenial and as a result I have an occasional fit of the blues which I feel as though nothing could cure but the presence of one far away. Tonight my thoughts wander back far into the happy past to that winter's school when you and I first knew and loved each other as boy and girl – Those were days of joy because of innocence I saw but the bright side of life. Today the dark obtrudes itself. Could you but be with me tonight. How that darkness would vanish, every thing would be forgotten in the happiness of the present.

Could I but feel your arms around my neck, your loving kiss upon my lips. Than this no earthly boon do I so much desire.

Was intending to write more but have been interrupted for two hours by a R.R. paymaster who desired to use the office to pay of the men who have but just left the premises and it is now very late and I must postpone a synopsis of my personal & family affairs until next time. Thanks for photo. Address same as before.

While Alva penned his love letters to Clara, Dane kept the residents of Black Earth informed about the wonders of the Colorado Springs area:

The Advertiser, Sept. 7, 1871
Overland Correspondence
Colorado Springs, Col., Aug. 15, 1871

Most every visitor from those states where they can never, by natural avenues, attain an altitude of but a few hundred feet above the sea level are ambitious when entering a mountainous region, to ascend one of the highest peaks.

To those who cast their anchors in this portion of Colorado, the rugged crests of Pike's Peak is the point to which their aspirations ascend. This peak, though not the highest, is the most widely known of any peak in the Rocky Mountains. It attained an historic note by being associated with the great gold discoveries of '59. This is an error of which it is difficult to determine its origin: no important gold discoveries having been made within a hundred miles of the peak, nor was it scarcely, if at all, visible to those crossing the plains impelled by their golden expectations.

Of the many who came here determined to gaze upon the wonderful panorama to which the ascent of Pike's Peak is the entrance fee, but a small minority succeed. With many, their desires evaporate, or are at least obscured, by the mere narration of the obsticles to be contended, of the physical labor and consequent fatigue that must be endured. Others succumb with the first few hours' journey, regarding it as a thing, to them, unattainable. Amid the many conflicting reports of the practability and impractability of the route, of the unattractiveness and of the fascinating beauty of the scenery, our interest was excited, our desires aroused, and we began to prepare for the undertaking. Our outfit consisted of two blankets and three days rations per man. Our journey was inaugurated with feelings more determined than boyant for it required but a short time to prepare us to fully corroberate any report that we had heard concerning the ladder-like — without the round (rung or crossbar) — character of the trail.

Our direction was along a mountain stream, which we were to follow to its source among the snow banks of the peak. In following our canyon, to avoid some perpendicular wall we were compelled to ascend the almost perpendicular mountain side, clinging to the vines and bushes for support and assistance, and again descending with the disagreeable sensation that every step downward must be again retaken. The second mile of our journey in which the stream has a decent of over two thousand feet, possesses more grandeur, more beauty of scenery than is ever in many an entire life. It is a continuation of cascades and falls, between walls that sometimes rises many hundred feet, over which some former convulsions of nature had cast granite boulders of immense proportions forming numerous and extensive caverns, in several of which the water coming through an aperture at the top forms a perfect fall of many feet, the effect is beautifully strange and fascinating. The echoing sound generated by the subterranean waters combined with their weird aspect in the dim and uncertain light awakens our admiration and wonder. But our Shekinah is beyond and we cannot linger. Five miles of circulous travel brings us to the top of the foot hills, where we enter a mountain park with the wild meadow grass five feet in height; but here, on account of innumerable fallen trees, locomotion was a most torturous proceeding, far more difficult than climbing the mountain side. Three miles of this tedious route brought us to the upper base of the peak, where it raises its silvery head far above its companions. Here, hungry and exhausted, we camped for the night, devoured our provender with infinite relish, built a large fire as sentinal to guard us from the approach of ravenous beasts, and amid the howling of cyots and the distant cry of the panther, reposed ourselves to sleep, to prepare for the labors of the morrow.

Early dawn found us prepared for our onward and upward journey. The air was now growing preceptibly lighter, rendering respiration difficult and "rests" necessary at the end of every few rods, our luggage, which upon starting weighed but fifteen pounds now seemed augmented into an immense burden.

Our approach to the timber line (over 11,000 feet above the sea) was indicated by the gradual diminuation of the height of the pine and cedar, which finally terminated in a line of scraggy, stunted and dead trees, which had long continued the battle against nature – a struggle between the bonded vassal and the despot – but it was a fight against destiny. The monarch's wind and storm, with their ruthless blade, severed every aspiration to cast their verdent branches beyond the confines of the immediate protecting rocks. Sapping their life blood and casting them back into a dwarfed insignificance to creep along the earth or to die. Typical of human despotism, which ever strangles with the galling manacles of tyranny those asperations which reach beyond the confines of ignorance, out into that pure domain of knowledge and free thought, whose atmosphere is pregnant with human freedom and equality.

Before us arose the barron peak, seeming by its very abruptness to defy any nearer approach. But as it is the last charge that decides the battle, the last quarter that determines the race, we struggled on with renewed energy

In 1871, Adams stepped onto the summit of Pikes Peak, completing a thrilling climbing adventure. (Colorado Springs Convention and Visitors Bureau)

and after three hours of toil, lay in a snow bank that crowned with its mantle of purity the apex of Pike's Peak. Fourteen thousand three hundred and twenty-six feet above the sea. The goal was reached. The struggle was ended. The cost had been great, but the reward was ample. A grander panorama no man could desire to see. Far to the east the level plain merged into the distant sky. To the north nothing but a succession of rugged mountains met the eye. Visible upon the western horizon were the snow clad mountains of Utah. To the south loomed the Spanish Peaks, and beyond lay the plains of New Mexico. To the north-west, South Park — one of the greatest natural parks in the world — flashed upon our vision, rich and beautiful in its gently undulating hills of wavey green. But that which, on account of its immediateness is the most entrancing, is the picturesqueness of the surrounding mountains and the ravishing beauty of a cincture of crystal pure water lakes which surround the upper base of the peak. Nature's diamonds circled in a radiant band around this queen of mountains.

These scenes are beyond the grasp of language, no words can faithfully portray them or convey a true idea of their magnificence. One must himself see them, or remain forever in ignorance of their grandeur and beauty. We would fain linger, for every moment unfolds new beauties, new points of admiration: but our time is limited and other points demand our attention. The top of the peak has an almost level surface of about one hundred acres, an extensive field of immense granite boulders. We played "boy" by

rolling boulders down an ice canyon of several thousand feet in length,
down which they flew with the rapidity of a cannon ball, flying into a thou-
sand fragments from their own velocity.

Several extinct craters exist, one of which is still several hundred feet in
diameter and as many deep, yet conveys an imperfect idea of their former
dimensions. Man's admiration is here converted into a reverential awe. He
feels his own significance as his thoughts ascend to the Great Author of all
these wonders, who long ages ago touched this mount and made it to smoke
and cast forth its torrents of fire. It is an interesting problem for the geolo-
gist and antiquarian, to determine the period of the volcanic era of the
Rocky Mountains. When these mountains greeted each other with their
floods of fire and lava. Many relics of former visitors was found, one of
which bore the following inscription: "To whom it may concern: This certi-
fies that I, William Hardin, of El Paso Co., Col., arrived at day-light on
the 10th day of July, 1871, and if ever caught here again at four o'clock in
the morning, may I be apprehended as a fit candidate for the lunatic asy-
lum." On the top of a mighty constructed monument we found the cards of
two adventurers, encased in a bottle, which gave indications that their spir-
its had departed on their journey up. After plucking a few alpine flowers
and mosses as they peeped out from their snowy beds, we commenced the
descent, and upon our arrival at the foot of the mountains, experienced no
surprise that the man who had twice ascended Pike's Peak was still a
curiosity belonging to the future.

Dane[36]

In spite of Alva's apparent elation over his new surroundings, the
Adams family was still plagued by troubles. In September, Alva shared his
worries with Clara on stationery with a letterhead of the "Office of the
Fountain Colony, Colorado Springs, Col.," complete with a map of the
Denver and Rio Grande Railway. Clara's full name was Marie Clara Heeney,
which explains the salutation "M.C.H." [37]

Colorado Springs, Col., Sept. 18, 1871
   M.C.H.,
   Our large family is rapidly diminishing. Of nine children but five remain.
George left us last Tuesday, yet I cannot mourn the poor boy as I ought. I
cannot but feel that it is better so. His sufferings are over. His troubles past.
At most he was ill prepared to battle the realities of life. Better now lay down
the cross and be at rest than struggle on only to drink deeper of human bitter-
ness — to experience more and more the anguish of disappointment.
Fortunately Father arrived Saturday night before George died. He left here

this morning for home (and) he remains in Denver until the later part of the week where Mother and Frank, Libbie and Willie will meet him to proceed home together. Father wanted me to take a trip with him through the mountains and mines but as Sanborn is absent I was compelled to remain here and attend to business. There is a new firm in this place Sanborn and Adams by name who are erecting the largest store in this part of the Territory to be run in connection with a Lumber Yard. What think you? Are we nearer each other or farther apart? Much nearer think I. It was a struggle for me to give up my expected vacation even temporarily as I hope it is. But health was the consideration that finally influenced me. Dollars alone would have had no effect. John remains with me. Homesick as I have been I expect to be still more lonesome when Mother leaves. But look forward to the time when one that cometh will put away all such sensations and in the companionship of one, I will want no more. Do not let the brevity of this disappoint you, will do better next time. Have been writing about a dozen business letters and to use an expression more forcible than elegant, I am "played out." Write immediately.

With many kisses,
AA

The residents of Black Earth, Wisconsin, also learned the sad news of George's death:

The Advertiser, Sept. 21, 1871

DIED. ADAMS – in Colorado City, Tuesday afternoon, September 12, 1871. George Adams, aged 18 years, 8 months and 19 days.

DEATH OF GEORGE ADAMS – By a private letter from Alva Adams, dated at Colorado City, Tuesday the 12th, we receive the sad intelligence of the death of his brother, George, that afternoon. Their father arrived there the Saturday before. The sad news of George's death is received with sorrow by his many friends here.

Although the death of George soured the Colorado trip, there had been many pleasant occurrences. One of Libbie Adams' fond memories was the batch of biscuits her mother made when they camped at the soda springs, using the natural soda water. Libbie was disappointed, however, that George had not camped with them at Manitou, staying instead in a two-story boarding house in Colorado City.

Libbie also described the family's situation at the time of her brother's death:

Alva seemed to be the more frail, and there would have been no surprise if he had gone, but George took ill very suddenly. . . . When we saw that he could not get well Father came on by train and took Mother and the rest of us back, all but Alva and John.

Father left the three teams and all the equipment with Alva, and some ready money, all of which was paid back, but the various "hard luck" stories of his hauling railroad ties was largely imaginary. A man with three good teams and strong, new wagons was able to make close to $10 a day, which was affluence in 1871. The teamsters probably loaded and unloaded the ties, and Alva drove one of the wagons. Moreover, he did not continue to haul ties very long for he went into business in Colorado Springs almost as soon as the town was laid out.[38]

The September 28, 1871, edition of the *Advertiser* announced that Mr. and Mrs. John Adams and the three smaller children had returned to Black Earth from Colorado on the afternoon of the 26th. Sons Alva and John were reported to have remained at Colorado Springs. Alva was "preparing to engage in the furniture and hardware business. The family come back somewhat improved in health."

Alva continued to write to Clara. He was angry because a recent letter he had written her had been returned unclaimed. Still recovering from his brother's death, apparently experiencing mixed emotions regarding Clara's reaction to his decision not to become an attorney, and having been forced to give up a planned vacation for reasons of health, he penned this poignant letter. Adams also was trying to cope with his absent business partner, who was deep in mourning over the death of his wife:

Sent a letter to you through Hattie Hill ten days ago which had been returned to me from Chicago. How was it? Did you upon the receipt of one fail to call again not expecting more? The overthrow of my legal asperations I regret very much. But the question had resolved itself to the following: To be something else and live or be a lawyer and die. Between the two alternatives after long discussing the question with myself I finally decided against my desires. Circumstances that was considerable to my credit cast my lines in this direction (Lumber etc). Nor do I join in your surprise in my choosing this vocation, it being a business that pays as well as any. Is not disagreeable and is healthy. Our business affairs have been greatly affected lately over the calamities of my partner whose wife died some weeks ago which affected him so that he was "Non Compos" for several weeks and is still unable to pay much attention to business. Expect him down here tomorrow when we have a settlement from which time this institution will be known under the style and firm of Alva Adams Lumber Furniture and Hardware etc Dealer. Physicaly I am improving. Have increased my avoirdupoise 15 lbs during the past month — and can now raise the beam at over 150. How is that for substantiality? Financialy I have likewise been quite successfull for since my entrance in the Ter (Territory) by hard days work and some head work I supported the family while here and am now probably ten or twelve hundred ahead. If I could only continue in that ratio I would be satisfied but there is many chances and in a week I may lose all. Have no fear of my ever attaching to much value to "Stamps." It would be fortunate for me did I value it more and had I have done so more during the past five years I might have preserved quite a handsome amount from the dollars squandered during that time. Excuse my enlarging upon my private affairs but knowing you had a curiosity to hear of them I have thought best to gratify it. Write often. Did you know how welcome were your letters to me and how much good they do me, you would write oftener. With a question I close. How long before you will come to remain forever to the arms of your loving A?

Another letter to Clara from Alva was torn, with the right side of the front page and the top of the back side of the page missing. Half sentences have little meaning except to convey that Alva was unhappy, and that Clara had ripped off half of his letter after reading it. The few remaining words seem to ask Clara if she did not receive his last letter. And if she had not yet written, she should do so immediately! All that was left of the torn date was "Sunday Oct.":

. . . .whom it is meant. Recd a letter from our Mutual "Hattie." She appears to be perfectly enraptured with her journey and visit. It is a calamity that we have not more true hearted girls like Hattie Hill Have just begun to appreciate her worth and cannot feel too thankfull that she did not cast me off when I gave her every provocation to do so. As I have likewise to others of whom I thought the most. Father and Mother are about to Kansas City tonight and will arrive at B.E. about Tuesday night. Expect I shall have occasion to go to Chicago next Spring at which time, if I do not remain, will make a visit to my old homes (Bandellus?) and Black E.

It is getting late and I must cease. Shall expect a long letter in return as well as one for the letter sent some days since. Could you but be with me tonight as in the photo which I have before me I fear that my inclination to sleep would not be very imperative until the wee small hours, at least. Oh for a few hours of the days that are past or of the days that are to come.

Yours through fate,

A

Clara Heeney at age 18.
(MacGregor Ranch)

Chapter Three

CLARA

I n the fall of 1871, while Alva Adams was struggling and lonely in Colorado Springs, Clara Heeney went to Chicago to study landscape painting at the Chicago Academy of Design, a school later to become the Art Institute. On October 8 of that year, 18,000 buildings in the lakefront metropolis were destroyed in the great Chicago fire, leaving 90,000 people homeless. The magnificent new Academy of Design building completed the previous year was destroyed, along with all of its casts and a 300-piece collection of paintings. Crosby's Opera House, decked out for its October 9 opening with $80,000 worth of new upholstery, frescoes and ornaments ($5,000 on French bronzes alone), also was consumed by the flames. To the realm of art, the fire was a staggering loss that took almost a decade to recoup.

Although Clara was in Chicago at the time, no details of her experiences during the fire are known. Not until 10 days later did she make any entries in her small 1870-1871 diary: "Ruins, Ruins, all Chicago is in ruins. Twenty four hours laid waste to the work of a lifetime. What a grand night."

While "grand night" may seem an odd choice of words in describing such an extensive and destructive fire, other accounts of the event included similar verbiage. In his recollections, the former lieutenant governor of Illinois, William Bross, referred to it as a "wonderful event." When the fire was at its height, he described it as "the most grandly magnificent scene that one can conceive."

Shortly after the fire, Clara received a letter from Alva written on stationery with the same letterhead of the "Office of the Fountain Colony." The mention of "John" in the letter presumably referred to Alva's brother, not quite 17 years old. He had remained at Colorado Springs with Alva when the rest of the family returned to Black Earth.

Colorado Springs, Col., Oct. 25, 1871

> *Mine own (erasure, underlining still visible),*
> *After many days of anxiety and innumerable calls at the post office I*

was today, after a silence of five or six weeks, the happy recipiant of your letter. All my fears were immediately dissipated as to the dangers that you might have incured in the burning of Chicago and I am tonight the happiest chap in this ambryo city. You cannot imagine the exhilerating effect produced upon a boy by the receipt of a letter from his lady love, especially when he has been long expecting it.

You repeat my desire when wishing you could step into my office. Here I am all alone. John & Charlie – Hired man – have gone over to the board- ing house to make an evening call. . . . The landlord has a very handsome daughter. Hour 9 p.m. What visions of happiness arise even with the thought of your being here with me. But they are visions only for many a long mile intervene between you and I who should be here together heart- to-heart. How much happier, stronger, would I be and I believe that you too, dear girl, who has had so much to contend, so much of disappointment and sorrow to meet, would be happier here with me. What think you? Is it not true? Have been building a little cottage merely to have comfortable bachelor quarters. Yet all the people here attribute my actions to other motives. They all believing that I am but preparing to bring a better half out here to console me through the coming winter. They also think that the event is not far distant. Would that I could verrify their predictions. But they poor fools know not that another hand than mine has gauged the time and that by them the happy day has been fixed many months – even years – in the future. What mean you by your reference to a Wisc wife? Am get- ting exceeding dull and could not determine whether you were quizing me or whether you were relenting in your self assumed obligation. Which was it? I know my hopes upon the question but will not express them until I hear your decision.

While Alva penned these letters that gave clear evidence of Clara's changing feelings, Clara was busy and happy in Chicago. Her autograph album[39] furnished evidence that her class occasionally met at academy founder Henry Crawford Ford's Riverside, Illinois, residence after the fire destroyed the school. During these meetings, plans undoubtedly were discussed for a sketching tour to the Colorado Rockies during the summer of 1872. The young artists in the class would be challenged to help capture a pictorial record of the Old West. Ford also had enthralled the art students with tales of his own experiences on a tour to the Rockies in 1866. He awakened in them a pioneering spirit, a sense of adventure and a desire to explore the unknown.

With two other Chicago artists, H.A. Elkins and J.F. Gookins, Ford, his wife and their baby had joined an emigrant wagon train from Omaha for quite an adventurous trip over the Great Plains. A "hurricane"– no doubt a tornado – took down their tents and blew over heavily loaded wagons near Cottonwood, Nebraska. Fort Cottonwood, located on the Mormon Trail, later would be known as Fort McPherson.

A letter from Gookins explained, "Ford says that just as he was crawling out of the tent his ears were saluted by a piercing wail and the pathetic cry of 'Oh, have you seen my baby!' He looked back and saw the tent down with his wife under it, turned his head, and lo!, over went our wagon with the horses down under it; and here was a woman before him wringing her hands and screaming for her baby." Though all were badly frightened, no one was seriously injured.[40]

Some of Ford's stories were equally thrilling, yet less frightening. After hearing many yarns from its mentor, the class was eager to take the sketching trip into the frontier. Clara's mother, Georgianna Heeney, agreed to accompany the group as a chaperone. The sketching tour proved to be an extraordinary experience for Clara.

As fate would have it, during the summer of 1872, when Alva and Clara's relationship had reached an uneasy stage, Clara Heeney was to meet her future husband, Alexander Quiner MacGregor. He was on a camping trip in Colorado during Clara's sketching tour with her art class. According to MacGregor Ranch legend, Clara and Alex were believed to have met in the Estes Park area the summer of 1872. But it seems more likely that Alex and Clara met near South Park.

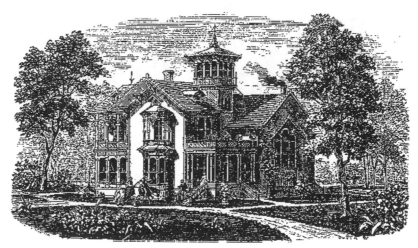

H.C. Ford's ornate, Swiss-styled Chicago home hosted Clara's art class after the great fire destroyed the art school. (Newberry Library, Chicago)

Reaching Estes Park in 1872 was an immense, very difficult undertaking. The area still was primitive, with poor trails, troublesome transportation and a lack of facilities. Isabella Bird's 10 hours of hard riding in 1873 to reach Estes Park on horseback, described in her book, *A Lady's Life in the Rocky Mountains,*[41] makes it seem less likely that H.C. Ford would have brought his students to that destination. Not until Alexander MacGregor's toll road was opened on July 28, 1875, was Estes Park's isolation finally brought to an end.

Further evidence that Alex and Clara met in South Park is furnished by the dates and locales of her oil paintings during the trip to Colorado.[42] But what might be the most convincing evidence appeared in the September 4, 1872, *Rocky Mountain News*. Alex reportedly departed on a "trip to the mountains, South Park and other sections with a fellow member of the Odd Fellows, his associate, Judge Bromwell."

Both Clara and her mother were enthused with Alex's positive views on Denver and the developing frontier. Realizing how much they enjoyed Colorado and the Rocky Mountains (and perhaps Alex himself), the two women decided to make a permanent move to Denver after the art trip, thinking the city would be an excellent location for Clara to open her studio.

On November 16, 1872, Clara placed the following ad in Denver's *Rocky Mountain News:*

This photo of mile-high Denver looking northwest from Broadway was taken in the late 1870s. (Denver Public Library)

LANDSCAPE PAINTING

Miss Clara Heeney, former pupil of H.C. Ford, president Chicago Academy of Design, will open a studio in Reithmann's block about December 1. Pupils solicited. For terms, etc., P. O. lock box 222.

Boarding with her mother, Clara opened her studio and became better acquainted with Alex MacGregor, the young Denver law clerk soon to become an attorney.

While Clara was experiencing mixed emotions over her future with Alva – it appears the two did not get together during her Colorado trip – it was apparent that she was beginning to feel secure and happy in her relationship with Alex. The evidence suggests that Alex and Clara admired one another. Alex was ambitious and intelligent. He must have found Clara interesting and bright, and found it pleasant to have conversations with her, listening to her notions and sentiments. Alex was determined to pursue Clara and keep in touch with her. They were able to spend much time together, getting to know each other's thoughts, beliefs, attitudes and aspirations. He appreciated her, and encouraged her to talk about her hopes for the future. He must have respected and given a lot of weight to her opinions for he ended up treating her like a full partner in his businesses.

Shortly before Clara's advertisement ran in the Denver paper, Alva Adams was in Black Earth on a visit from Colorado Springs. The newspaper announced that he was looking exceedingly well, and that he reported being pleased with his new home: "Alva has a large circle of friends here, and we hope that he may be induced to remain among us for some time. While North, he will visit Chicago, Milwaukee and Oshkosh, at which places he will purchase supplies for his hardware and furniture establishment in Colorado Springs."

The September 19, 1872, *Advertiser* announced that Alva Adams had started on his return to Colorado Springs "last Tuesday." Edwin Warner had accompanied him. "He goes to Colorado to do the tinkering for its citizens, and Alva in particular. Success go with them."

Alva's late-summer visit to Black Earth only widened the chasm developing between him and Clara. Not only had Clara previously been upset to learn that Alva had shared one of her letters with his cousin, Tom, but it seemed that Clara's apparent disappointment over Alva's discarding of his plans for a law career had compounded the problems.

Perhaps foremost in her concerns were rumors that Alva had flirted extensively with a Black Earth girl named Valinda Barnes. No letters from Clara to Alva have been located, and there is no record of meetings between the two during this period in their fracturing relationship. An acquaintance from Black Earth may have written to Clara hinting that Adams paid too much attention to this other young woman during his visit. But perhaps more significantly, Alexander MacGregor had come into Clara's life, and he may have been responsible for her change of affection.

A faint embossed seal which includes a crown accentuates the letterhead of this undated letter from Alva to Clara, one evidently written after their broken engagement, probably in October, 1872. It reveals the severing of their alliance:

Cannot comprehend the entire meaning which you intended to convey by those lines, given one. But you were right thus far "That your memory will be ever present to me" for years must pass and scenes must change ere we can eradicate from our minds the memory of those we love. This sentiment when once aroused adheres through all the vicissitudes of life in prosperity & adversity – in joy & sorrow, from youth til age. Many have I seen, with some have I been intimate, but through all have I been loyal to my first allegience. My conduct, I admit, may have at times appeared at varience to this statement, but it is true. But now that bond is broken. Our relations of the past are sundered, for what reasons I am ignorant. It is well, for today I am not what I was three months ago. Then I had hopes, ambitions. When two years had passed I had thought to have a profession of my own, to be prepared to enter upon the arena of life, to become a man among men. Today my affairs present a change, though not discouraged, still am I somewhat dispondent. A year or more of life must be sacrificed to health – and that period the seed time of the most bountiful harvest of life. Thus that point which a short time ago appeared so near has through the adversity of circumstances receded until it is almost obscured in the dim future. These prospects I would desire to entail upon no one. Your sundering of our ties.

(Erased section, barely visible)

In regard to my past conduct I desire to say that many of my actions appeared reprehensible which were not so in reality. I make no pretentions to perfection, any misdeeds have been by far too numerous, but my greatest crime has been the contempt and disregard in which I have held the opinions of some whom I dispised and to whom I can attribute the origins of some of my worst deeds, nor do I know that I desire to obliterate these pages from my past history, for those follies which I have committed will serve as pilots to preserve me from the shoals of the future. This is the last time that I shall intrude my troubles and afflictions upon you. Should not have done so now had I not thought them not entirely devoid of interest to you (illegible words). God bless you and give you that happiness which you deserve, is the prayer of

AA

Soon after Clara and Alva's broken engagement – the reason for the breakup never was fully understood – Alva married a lovely young woman he had met either in Greeley or Colorado Springs. The date was October 26, 1872. His bride was Ella Nye from Bangor, Maine, who had moved to Colorado with her family and lived in Greeley at the time Alva, his mother and the five younger siblings arrived by covered wagon.

In November, Hattie Hill, a dear friend of both Clara and Alva, wrote to Clara in shock over the disturbing news that Alva and Clara had broken their engagement, and that Adams had married someone else. This portion of the letter expresses her dismay:

177 Seventh St.
Milwaukee, Nov. 4, 1872
 My dear Clara,
 I did not "faint," today when reading yr. letter – but I could not believe my own eyes – I read – and re-read – Allie married!! can it be true? O! no-it-must-be you have had a dream! Dont tell me my dear girl that he has been so foolish as to go and marry a strange young lady/strange to me I mean. What does it all mean? You speak in Riddles to me – You said in yr. other letter that "You were to blame" – May I ask – did you refuse to engage yr. self to him? O: how could you my dear Clara – my dear Allie, it seems as if I must write him a few lines this very night – but no I must not – O! it's too late, nothing has ever affected me more than this – no – not even my own affairs – I never thought – he would do so – but What is Man? and he that I thought so noble, so honorable just like the rest of humanity – If we were only together this one night – even – how I do want to see you – I am lonely here – you are there – I know you are by the tone of your letters – but the same dear kind Father watches over us both – what should we do if we could not go to Him – when are hearts are almost breaking. He loves us – and will carry us safely through – if we only trust in him – I feel so sad – so bad – I cant write – its almost impossible – for I have so long hoped and thought that some day along in the future, all would be well – & you two – my dear friends – would be one – why I cant see how this ever happened – Which of you "did it" – so to speak/I felt very much grieved to think Allie did not come to see me. . . .
 That letter that you sent here to me for him I sent as I heard he was in

*B.E. — on one corner of the envelope I wrote (very fine) Please write —
H.I.H. 177 7th St. Mil — Did he ever receive the letter do you know? Do
you mean to say he married the young lady that was engaged to an Eastern
gentleman? You speak of going to the Hotel to call on them — Are you as
good friends as you were? Clara How strange this is — And "he left word
for you to call" — how queer it all is — Then it was not Valinda Barnes
after all — Wonder what she tells now — B.E. will have something new.*

(no signature)

*Known for her sincerity and kindliness, Ella Nye Adams proved a popular first
lady during Alva Adams' two full terms as governor. (Colorado Historical Society)*

News of Alva's wedding was printed in the *Advertiser* on November 7, 1872:

THANKS – We have received from Colorado City, Col., cards bearing the inscription, Mr. and Mrs. Alva Adams, Miss Ella Nye, which leads us to the conviction that Alva has went, and gone and done it, and committed matrimony. Well, they all will do it sooner or later. Here's our hand, and best wishes for Alva and his bride.

There were no travel columns from Dane after Adams' broken engagement to Clara Heeney and subsequent marriage. Clara asked Alva to return the photograph she had given him. Alva's belated answer was on stationery bearing the letterhead of "Adams, Wilson & Co., General Dealers in Builders' Hardware, Nails, Sash, Doors, etc., South Pueblo, Col."

South Pueblo, Col., Feb. 5, 1873

Clara,

Pursuant to promise I send you the photo. Have just found it else you would have had it sooner, so do not think me forgetfull of your request on account of the seeming delay.

Charlie and I make this place our headquarters at present. Ella has been in Greeley for two weeks so that I am again enjoying, temporarily, the beauties of single blessedness (Billiards etc).

Enjoying the salubrity of our Italian clime. We favored mortals of the south can afford to sympathize with the ice bound subjects of our northern province of Denver. You are welcome to your share

Hoping that in your undertakings you may be crowned with that success which your talants and goodness deserve is the wish of

Alva

Alexander Quiner MacGregor. (MacGregor Ranch)

Chapter Four

A L E X

*U*ntil recently, very little was known of Alexander Q. MacGregor's lineage on his father's side, except that in Milwaukee on May 16, 1844, Alexander McGregor of Alburg, Vermont, married the former Margaret Goodwin Quiner of Connecticut, born November 30, 1813, the 10th of 13 children of the former Margaret S. Dorr and her husband, William Quiner. Entries written into the Quiner family *Bible* tracing Margaret's family back to the 1700s are part of the collection preserved today at MacGregor Ranch.

Research has revealed that the McGregors were highlanders on the west side of Scotland, claiming descent from a King Alpin, who lived about 500 A.D. Unfortunately, their land was coveted by the Campbells, who were in full favor with the King of England. As a result, the McGregors were denied the use of the family name for almost 100 years, or they could choose to leave Scotland. Subsequently, a number of the McGregors became very successful outlaws during this period. When the ban of the use of the name was lifted, many McGregors emerged from behind other names.

Alexander Quiner MacGregor's great grandfather was Duncan McGregor, born in Scotland in 1755. Duncan was a British soldier in the American Revolution, a sergeant, according to the Haldimand papers, Canadian records of British soldiers who served in the Revolutionary War. After the war, he was rewarded with a British land grant of 500 acres in Canada for his service to the King. When the international line between Canada and the United States was settled in 1783, his land turned out to be two miles south of the Canadian border, in what is now Alburg, Vermont. After several years of litigation, the settlers in this area retained the lands given them by the British government and became American citizens.

Duncan McGregor Jr. (1781-1877)[43] was born in Montreal and moved to the family home in Alburg when he was less than a year old. He served at the battle of Plattsburgh, New York, in the War of 1812, and when offered a pension for his service, declined it. Alexander McGregor, the father of Alexander Quiner MacGregor, was the seventh of the 11 or 12 children of Duncan Jr. and his wife, the former Eleanor Burghardt.[44]

Tragic family circumstances preceded the March 4, 1846, birth of

Alexander Quiner MacGregor in Milwaukee, Wisconsin Territory. His older brother died at birth in March, 1845. Four months before Alex was born, his father drowned, along with his mother's brother, Henry Quiner, when the schooner Ocean capsized in Lake Michigan. Alex was raised in Milwaukee by his widowed mother. Margaret McGregor must have received comfort and support from her own mother, Margaret Quiner, also widowed, who lived with her for a time, and from other Quiner family members who lived in or near Milwaukee.

No records of Alex's education have been located, but it is known that at the time of the 1860 census, the 14-year-old boy was working on a farm at nearby Wauwatosa, Wisconsin.

Margaret's surviving brothers, Edwin Bently Quiner and Elisha Cushman Quiner, both working in the printing industry, apparently encouraged young Alexander to become an apprentice printer. Alex was a printer in Milwaukee for the *Daily Wisconsin* from 1865, at age 19, until age 23, when he became the publisher of the *La Belle Mirror* in Oconomowoc. He held the position from June, 1869, to August, 1870. His associate, Daniel H. Sumner, was an attorney who boarded with Alex and his mother. Before deciding to strike out for the newer frontier, Alex must have discussed with his co-publisher the possibility of youthful MacGregor pursuing a legal career after his arrival in Colorado Territory.[45]

Alex's whereabouts are unknown from August, 1870, to sometime in 1871, when he chose to settle in Denver. Although he displayed souvenirs of China at his wedding reception in Black Earth during Christmas, 1873, no record of a passport has been located.

For some reason, Alex changed the spelling of his last name from "McGregor" to "MacGregor" when he moved to Denver. After relocating to Colorado, Alex MacGregor worked as a law clerk for Probate Judge Henry A. Clough.[46] Upon being admitted to the bar, he practiced law for a time with noted Denver attorneys H.P.H. Bromwell and E.B. Sleeth.[47] MacGregor was active in the Republican Party, served as secretary of the Denver Independent Order of Odd Fellows Lodge #4 and was a member of both the Denver Scouts cavalry organization and the Denver (volunteer) Fire Department's First Hook and Ladder, City Hall Station.

After Clara's trip west with her art class, she and Alex continued their new friendship through correspondence. The courtship blossomed. It is conceivable that they had become "engaged to be engaged," or at least they certainly were attracted to each other, when Clara and Georgianna returned to their hometown of Black Earth in late April of 1873. They wouldn't be away from Colorado for too long, though. Alex and Clara would wed and make their dreams of a home in the West come true.

The edition of the *Black Earth Advertiser* just before Christmas, 1873, mentioned that "A.Q. MacGregor, a rising young attorney of Denver, Col., was now visiting friends here" and had paid a brief call to the *Advertiser* the previous Saturday.

A week later, the paper carried the story of Clara and Alex's wedding, an event for which the relatives had been gathering. Married at the family home in Black Earth on Christmas Day, 1873, the couple journeyed to Milwaukee and Chicago on their wedding trip and returned to Denver, where they had decided to make their home for the time being:

The Advertiser, Jan. 1, 1874

RECEPTION

Another of Black Earth's fair daughters have been captured and carried away to share the blessings of a happy married life.

Miss M. Clara Heeney, one of our most talented young ladies, was, on the twenty-fifth of December, united in marriage with a Mr. A.Q. MacGregor, a rising young member of the legal profession, of Denver, Col. The ceremony was conducted in a quiet way at the bride's home. Only a few relatives being present. On the evening following, a reception was given at which a large number of friends were present. The occasion was one of the most enjoyable. During the evening Mr. MacGregor showed to the company specimens of Chinese curiosities, such as ladies' shoes, chop sticks, coin, fruit & (so on), which, with his descriptions of Chinese life, were of much interest to the company. Mrs. MacGregor added interest and enjoyment to the occasion by showing many specimens of her skill as an artist, while Mrs. Heeney added no little to the occasion by displaying her cabinet of Colorado ores, agates, stones, petrified wood, etc.

And then there was the supper. Really we feel inadequate to express our admiration for a magnificent repast spread before the company; or the pleasant manner in which all were made to feel themselves at home by Mr. and Mrs. Carlos Burton. The occasion was one long to be remembered by all who participated.

The happy couple will extend their homeward trip by the way of Milwaukee and Chicago, at which cities they will linger a few days. They carry with them the many good wishes for a long and happy union.

MARRIED

MACGREGOR-HEENEY — At the residence of Mr. Carlos Burton, of Black Earth, Dec. 25th, 1873, by Rev. M.M. Martin, of Mazomanie,

Alexander MacGregor wore many business hats in his new hometown of Estes Park, pictured here in the early 1900s. (Denver Public Library)

Mr. A.Q. MacGregor, of Denver, Colorado, and Miss M. Clara Heeney, of Chicago.

May the harmony and good cheer which was manifested on their wedding evening, be but a fitting prelude to their married lives.

M.M.M[48]

Prospects were bright for the newly wed Alex. In addition to working as an attorney, MacGregor would become a surveyor and builder of a toll road between Estes Park and the vicinity of Lyons. He developed a sawmill, built an ice house and a meat house and applied for a patent for his method of preserving fresh fowl, meat and fish. He was a homesteader, cattle rancher, cobbler, government weather observer and road builder. He operated a freighting and transportation business. He served as the first notary public of Estes Park[49] and was an early banker, making loans before there was a bank in the area. He developed a resort for tourists and later became a justice of the peace and a judge. MacGregor is also remembered for his role in joining the fight against the Estes Park area becoming the private domain of a wealthy European newcomer known as Earl of Dunraven.

The governor's family (from right): Alva, Ella and Alva Blanchard, the couple's only surviving child. The boy later would go on to a successful political career of his own. (Colorado Historical Society)

Chapter Five

ALVA AND ELLA

*I*n 1872, Alva took J.C. Wilson into partnership in the hardware business at his Colorado Springs store. Adams and his wife, Ella, moved to the new town of South Pueblo, Colorado, opening a branch store there in what is now the greater Pueblo area. He was chosen a trustee of South Pueblo in 1873. From his modest beginning, Alva rapidly increased his trade and capital. He was able to open a fine store in Del Norte in 1875, profited by a large trade with the San Juan country and afterwards, opened other branches in that district.

But life still could be unkind to Adams. Edna, Alva and Ella's first child, was born in Pueblo in 1873. She lived only three weeks, dying on September 28.

The *Advertiser* informed its readers on October 30, 1873, that Alva's father, John Adams, had sold his interest in his Black Earth store. In late winter, the newspaper published more information regarding Alva's business:

The Advertiser, Feb. 12, 1874

PERSONAL – Mr. Alva Adams is back from Colorado, visiting his parents. He stops but a few days, when he goes on to New York, where he intends to purchase his spring stock of hardware and miner's outfits for their store in El (Del) Norte, Col. We are pleased to learn of Alva's prosperity. The improvement of his health alone has been full compensation for his time spent there, even if he had not succeeded in bettering his financial condition.

Again spotlighting the Adams family, the July 23, 1874, *Advertiser* announced that Sheriff John Adams' family departed for Colorado "last Monday morning, taking with them a God speed from many friends and neighbors." This was apparently just a visit to Colorado, not a relocation. John Adams served as sheriff of Dane County in 1874-1875, and once again was elected to the Wisconsin State Senate in 1882. John, being an influential Democratic leader, obtained and operated the Black Earth post office from 1886 to 1890. Libbie Adams virtually served as postmaster as her father was away most of the time looking after his Midwestern livestock businesses.

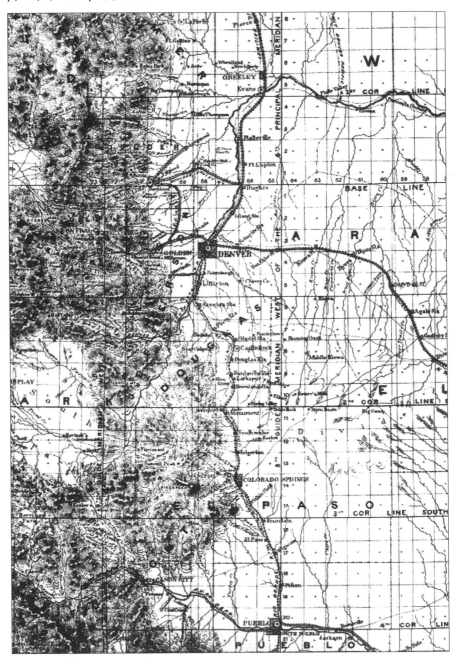

*Colorado still was wide-open country one year after the territory joined the Union.
The graphic above is the Front Range portion of a state map published in 1877.
(Denver Public Library)*

The September 24, 1874, *Advertiser* carried a final travel letter written earlier by Alva's father describing their trip to Colorado by train. It was a much easier trip than the one his family had taken by covered wagon three years earlier. John Adams, too, wrote as an anonymous correspondent, "J," describing the excursion from Black Earth to South Pueblo, Colorado, the home of son, Alva, and his family. John's wife, Eliza, probably daughter, Libbie, and likely one or two of Alva's younger brothers, probably John and Billy, were along on the trip.

When Alva and Ella's second and last child, Alva Blanchard Adams, was born on October 28, 1875, the family was living in Del Norte, the San Luis Valley mining community where one of the branch outlets for Alva's hardware and mining supplies stores was located. In 1876, when he was only 26, Alva was elected a member of the first Colorado Legislature, representing Rio Grande County.

Granted statehood the year of the centennial of the Declaration of Independence, Colorado had a population of approximately 180,000, with Denver as its urban keystone. The Centennial State had railroads, churches, schools, colleges, theaters, hospitals and other trappings Victorian Americans deemed essential parts of modern civilization. In an understandable outburst of boosterism, author Frank Fossett exclaimed, "Colorado has a population unsurpassed for intelligence, enterprise, thrift and energy; and this population is now of a settled and permanent character." Praising the law-abiding nature of the people, he concluded, "No state ever entered the Union with a people possessing an equal degree of culture, refinement and wealth. Less flamboyantly, agriculture had progressed markedly through the past seven years, drawing closer to fulfilling the needs of the local markets."[50]

Surely, Alva Adams, one of the first citizens of Colorado Springs, could be proud of his adopted state. His pride would only grow when he was elected its governor some years later.

Wild and beautiful, Estes Park stirred pioneer souls more than a century ago. This photo was taken in 1873 by William Henry Jackson. (U.S. Geological Survey)

Chapter Six

SETTLEMENT OF ESTES PARK

*A*uthor Clare Arthur's summation of a mountain valley's history recalled the Estes Park of years past:

Various Indian tribes were frequent visitors to the present-day Estes Park area, but never made this region a permanent settlement. A large number of explorers and trappers passed through the region, recording landmarks and naming mountains and rivers, yet it was not until October 1859 that anyone entered the area and decided to establish a permanent settlement. Joel Estes' short lived attempt to settle in Estes Park, from 1863 to 1866, ended when the family decided that a warmer climate was necessary for both their animals and themselves, and moved south. But during the years that the Estes family lived there, the area gained both notoriety and a name. Rocky Mountain News Editor William N. Byers attempted to scale Longs Peak and visited the Estes family during August 1864. Upon returning to Denver he wrote about the area he had named Estes Park, and encouraged others to visit there.[51]

Griffith J. Evans came to the Estes Park area as a squatter in the late 1860s and in 1867, he gained control of the Joel Estes property. In the fall of that year, Evans' friend, Captain George W. Brown of Longmont, offered to bring Evans, his wife, Jane, and their three children on the laborious 20-mile trip up the canyon to Estes Park to their new home. As Brown later recalled the story:

Mrs. Griff Evans came to me. . . . to tell me of such a splendid opportunity they had to go up to Estes Park and care for the Ranch of Jacobs (formerly the property of Joel Estes). Those were the days when a job was a job, but she said they had no way of getting there. As I had never visited the place, I offered to take them. I had a good stout wagon and team doing nothing just then. My offer was enthusiastically accepted, so the following morning I went over to see what they would have to move in the way of household goods. The list was short — a broken cook stove, two chairs past using, a table with one leaf gone, and a few pieces of bedding making up the entire list. After loading these onto the wagon, I said, "Now for the provisions." Mrs. Evans said, "We haven't any." It was the truth, they had nothing, and were ready to start to that lonely place at the beginning of winter with no supplies. I asked Griff what he meant to do. "Ain't there deer and fish?" was his answer. "Have you a gun?" I asked. "Yep." "Any powder?" "No." "Any anything?" "No.". . . So we passed our camp and I divided my supplies with them, a sack of measly little potatoes and one of smutty flour, a little powder and lead and salt. Thus replinished, we started for the famous Estes Park. I think I mentioned the condition of the furniture as none too good at the start. But after being rescued from three turnovers and finally deposited in the little log shack that comprised the only house in Estes, it was some worse. We found quite a lot of cattle about the place, and succeeded in catching two young calves. By putting them in the corral over night we were able, after quite some difficulties, to get some

Colorful, controversial Griff Evans was the father of Estes Park's tourism industry. (Estes Park Area Historical Museum)

milk from their mothers for the youngsters breakfast. After a day or two of inspection of the Park, I left the first Lyons family that ever moved to Estes to manage as best they could. Mind you, Griff had to carry his saddles of venison on his shoulder from Estes to the John Reece place on the St. Vrain to trade for any further supplies, a walk of some forty miles or more. At that, he made good, making his home there for many years, or until his boys were nearly grown. Later, the English Company bought out the Park.[52]

Evans moved to Colorado from Michigan in 1863. Although he soon made a small fortune, he lost it through a dishonest partner. According to an 1874 *Rocky Mountain News* account:

His sense of honesty compelled him to settle all claims against the firm, and not only his money, but his last team, went in this way. In this destitute condition, with his wife and their little children, he went to Estes Park some eight years ago (1867). Their journey was made on pack mules and when these returned, for he did not own even them, he was left in that wilderness with his gun and less than a dollar in money.[53]

In 1870, Evans may have built a stone house west of the present town of Lyons, near the North St. Vrain Creek. At one time, the house served as a stage stop and inn for travelers to Estes Park. According to another source, Griff Evans bought the house from a William Sites in 1877. For a period, Evans had residences in both the Estes Park and Lyons areas. He also held the distinction of being counted twice in the 1870 U.S. Census. He was listed in the St. Vrain District, Boulder County Census, as a laborer, having no property and no wife.[54] Meanwhile, the census taker for the Sherwood District, Larimer County, Post Office: Fort Collins, recorded that Evans, his wife, Jane, four children from ages 1 to 13 and James McLaughlin resided in a single dwelling in that district.

In March of 1872, a Longmont newspaper related:

Mr. G.J. Evans is down from Estes Park, and reports that stock up there has done well this winter. Out of eight hundred head wintered, only two or three were lost, and those by accident. Mr. Evans has just taken 75 head of beef cattle to market. The cattle found their own living among the hills, no hay being fed.[55]

Evans' family, like the women and children of many early pioneers, sometimes was sent down to the valley for the winter months, leaving Evans free, under such conditions, to return to the mountains periodically to check on his cattle and property. This seems, in fact, to have been the case during the latter part of Isabella Bird's stay in 1873, when as the only

Isabella Bird. (Denver Public Library)

woman in residence in Estes Park she boarded with Evans. Bird noted that the scenery was the most glorious she had ever seen, there were good meals, she had a clean hay bed with six blankets and there were "neither bugs nor fleas." Bird paid $8 a week, which included the unlimited use of a horse when one could be found and caught.[56]

Indefatigable Lady Isabella Lucy Bird (1831-1904) ranks among Estes Park's most famous visitors. This world-traveling adventurer arrived on horseback in October of 1873. In the words of her biographer, Pat Barr:

Isabella Bird belonged. . . . to that colourful band of travelling individualists of the late 19th century who, for all their eccentricities, had one feature in common — an innate, abiding, intensely emotional distaste for the constraints imposed by their own highly civilized society.[57]

In her book, *A Lady's Life in the Rocky Mountains*, one of the West's literary classics, Bird described the beauty of the Colorado mountain valley:

From the ridge on which this gulch terminates, at a height of 9,000 feet, we saw at last Estes Park, lying 1,500 feet below in the glory of the setting sun, an irregular basin, lighted up by the bright waters of the rushing Thompson, guarded by sentinel mountains of fantastic shape and monstrous size, with Long's Peak rising above them all in unapproachable grandeur, while the Snowy Range, with its outlying spurs heavily timbered, come down upon the park slashed by stupendous canyons lying deep in purple gloom. The rushing river was blood red, Long's Peak was aflame, the glory of the glowing heaven was given back from earth. Never, nowhere, have I seen anything to equal the view into Estes Park.[58]

Bird also was impressed by her host, remembering Griff Evans as "a splendid shot, an expert and successful hunter, a bold mountaineer, a good rider, a capital cook and a generally 'jolly fellow.'" Evans had become convinced by the numerous visitors to the mountain park that it would be profitable to offer food and lodging, and he added cabin after cabin to accommodate them.[59]

When the Earl of Dunraven came over Park Hill two days after Christmas in 1872, he and his party found Evans and the ranch house and several small cabins comprising the first dude ranch in Estes Park.[60] Dunraven, too, liked what he saw in Estes Park and soon would etch his name in local historical annals as the architect of the valley's epic 19th-century land grab.

This painting of Griff Evans' ranch was made in 1874. (Estes Park Area Historical Museum)

This aristocratic English earl was not an American citizen, much less a resident of Estes Park. Nor was he an "alien who had filed his first papers," the first step toward American citizenship. This did not discourage him from taking advantage of generally loose enforcement of the provisions in the 1862 Homestead Act. The homestead legislation granted 160 acres of agricultural land almost free to settlers who lived on the land and made substantial improvements on their newly acquired property. Dunraven, it is popularly believed, planned to accumulate vast amounts of land to be used as a private hunting preserve, maybe even a vast high country ranch. His development plans have been the subject of debate. His intentions have not. Windham Thomas Wyndham-Quin, better known as the Earl of Dunraven, wanted it all. According to one area historian:

> Dunraven, a wealthy Irish lord, came to the park on a hunting expedition in late December, 1872 and again in 1873 and 1874. Immediately enamored both with the scenery and the abundance of elk, deer, bighorn sheep, and other game, the earl soon launched an ambitious attempt to gain control of the park for a private hunting preserve. Dunraven consulted lawyers in Denver, who told him that in order to control and fence the park he must gain legal title to all lands on which there were springs or streams. To carry out this grand design Dunraven employed as his agent one Theodore Whyte. . . . who set about orchestrating the filing of claims (many of them fraudulent, as it turned out) under the federal Homestead Act of 1862.[61]

After having the area legally surveyed, which opened the land to

An aristocratic adventurer, the Earl of Dunraven attempted to gain control of most of Estes Park, possibly for use as a private hunting reserve. His efforts earned him widespread condemnation and later, praise for slowing development of the mountain valley. (Estes Park Area Historical Museum)

patent filings, Dunraven employed several accomplices boasting somewhat dubious backgrounds from nearby Front Range towns to stake claims under the Homestead Act. The earl's Estes Park Company Limited, also known as the English Company, subsequently would purchase the claims for a few dollars apiece. At one point, Dunraven reportedly controlled approximately 15,000 acres of the Colorado mountain valley.

The property improvements made by these "settlers" were no less suspicious than the method of acquisition, in the opinion of many observers:

Coming to the park, some of them laid up mere log foundations, others erecting small stockades, and some brush fencing small pieces of ground for suppositious garden spots. . . . By such nefarious means and illegal purchase, Dunraven secured some ten thousand acres of land, in fact nearly all of Estes Park proper, thus preventing actual worthy settlers from ever homesteading and more thickly populating the region.[62]

The Earl's activities drew the immediate attention of the Colorado press. One paper sounding the alarm was the *Fort Collins Standard*. According to the August 12, 1874, edition:

We are informed from reliable sources that one of the most villainous land steals ever perpetrated in Colorado has been enacted in Estes Park with the last few months, by some Englishmen, who through the perjury of various parties, have succeeded in gaining possession of some 6,000 acres of land lying, on either side of, and controlling the different streams in the Park.

Not surprisingly, battle lines were drawn between the valley's honest settlers and the men working for Dunraven. Emotions ran high. Acts of violence occurred. One of the more well documented involved one of the area's colorful characters, James Nugent, better known as Rocky Mountain Jim.

An early Estes Park settler, Nugent previously associated closely with Griff Evans. In 1868, when pioneer settler Abner Sprague and two companions first visited the area, they came across Evans and Rocky Mountain Jim working together, setting posts. Like other early settlers, Nugent made his living by trapping and raising a small herd of cattle. But it was his choice of real estate would prove pivotal to his fortunes. Anyone traveling the main route through Muggins Gulch into Estes Park passed near Nugent's cabin. And Jim would be no ally of the earl, choosing instead to harass British visitors intent on using the park as their own private hunting grounds.

Typical of many frontiersmen, Rocky Mountain Jim had a mysterious past, so conflicting in detail that it is almost impossible to construct his tale with accuracy. At various times, he described himself as the nephew of Confederate General P.G.T. Beauregard and hailing from the South, or as the son of a British army officer stationed in Canada. Nugent also claimed to have been an employee of both the Hudson's Bay Company and the American Fur Company. He told of having homesteaded in Missouri and fought with guerrilla forces in the Kansas border warfare. Reports even claimed he was a defrocked priest and a former schoolmaster.

Despite his rough edges and a face partially disfigured, Nugent left indelible impressions on more than one valley visitor. Recalled Isabella Bird, a Nugent admirer who climbed Longs Peak in the company of Rocky Mountain Jim in 1873:

Rocky Mountain Jim (was) an educated man who had come from eastern Canada too late to be a genuine "mountain man," but too early to earn a living as a dude wrangler. He told tales of his life as a fur trapper with Hudson's Bay Company, proudly exhibited a mutilated face won in a fight with a bear, recited classical poetry, talked intelligently on current topics, had a nimble wit and was a subtle tease. Mr. Nugent is what is known as "splendid company." [63]

Ill feelings developed between Griff Evans and Rocky Mountain Jim, probably over their differing opinions on the earl's land acquisition plans. But the possibility that Nugent made improper glances towards Evans' teenage daughter also may have been an important factor in the growing rift between the two men. The fire of their antagonisms may have been stoked by liquor. [64]

Evans also had been raised to believe in "class." He was of the laboring class, and thought himself equal to anyone in that category, but he would take off his hat and bow his very lowest to a man with wealth or title. In one opinion:

To have a chance to call a man "My Lord" and have that man claim to be his friend, pass him the bottle first, and call on that friendship to protect "My Lord" from a desperado in time of need, was Evans' undoing, and caused him to be a party to the first Estes Park tragedy — the killing of James Nugent. [65]

When Nugent was shot and mortally wounded in 1874, there were as many different versions of the circumstances as there were reasons for the shotgun slaying itself. In the opinion of one publication, "Fundamentally, it was the fault of the Earl of Dunraven. Griff Evans was the Earl's man, but Rocky Mountain Jim decidedly was not." [66] The most likely reason for the killing was Dunraven's wish to get rid of the valley's hostile gatekeeper, who had been said to have taken pot shots at trespassers. But Nugent did not go quickly or quietly. According to one recollection:

Lingering for months with a bullet in his skull, furious at being held in custody pending trial after the "shoot-out," [Nugent] wrote a long and eloquent letter to The Fort Collins Standard, August 21, 1874, which concluded: "Great God! Is this your boasted Colorado? That I, an American citizen who has trod upon Colorado's soil since '54 must have my life

attempted and deprived of liberty when the deep-laid scheme to take my life
has failed, and all for British gold!"

Rocky Mountain Jim[67]

Following the shooting, Griff Evans became a prime suspect. Evans
turned himself in to authorities at Fort Collins and gave his side of the
story. He was released, and soon left Estes Park, turning his residual Estes
Park holdings over to the English Company. Evans moved his family back
to the St. Vrain Valley and had a hand in opening the first of the area's great
stone quarries in partnership with Richard Smith and Edward S. Lyon, for
whom the nearby town of Lyons was named.

About 1883, Griff and Jane Evans moved back to the mountains,
relocating to Jamestown (northwest of Boulder) where for a number of
years, Evans owned and operated the Evans House hotel. Evans died at
Jamestown on July 6, 1900. He and Jane are buried there.[68]

Isabella Bird offered her own brief retort to the debate over who shot
Jim Nugent, and why: "Of the five differing versions which have been
written to me of the act itself and its immediate causes, it is best to give
none." If the lady whose heart and head were involved could not sort out
the truth, who can?[69]

By the mid- and latter 1870s, the steady stream of determined settlers
entering the Estes Valley convinced Dunraven that any dreams of a huge
hunting preserve were futile. Much of the earl's lands would be turned over
to cattle grazing, and the Englishman went on to play a major role in
developing the area's tourism industry. In 1877, the year after Colorado celebrated statehood, Dunraven opened his Estes Park Hotel. The mountain
valley now had its first true resort. (It would burn to the ground in 1911.)

Unlike days past when Dunraven's opposition was weaker and more
scattered, the area's new settlers put up stiff resistance to the earl's land
scheme. Alex MacGregor joined the chorus of dissent. His efforts culminat-
ed in a detailed letter written from Estes Park on July 23, 1881, to John
A. Jones, a special agent for the federal Department of the Interior in
Laramie, Wyoming.

In his letter, MacGregor noted that as soon as Dunraven's survey was
completed, 30 claims had been entered by persons completely unknown to
residents of Estes Park. Another, Alex said, was made by a former
MacGregor ranch hand who did not meet Homestead Act requirements and
had taken $100 from Theodore Whyte to submit the false filing. After
patents were granted on the 31 claims, the letter said, Whyte arranged
transfer of ownership into Dunraven's English Company.

(Top) The Earl of Dunraven's Estes Park hotel is believed to be the first resort hotel opened in Colorado. (Denver Public Library)... (Bottom) The hotel was destroyed by fire in 1911. (Denver Public Library)

In 1875, a grand jury investigation had resulted in perjury indictments against the 31 absentee homestead filers whose lands were in Dunraven's possession. The individuals could not be located and served court papers, and the indictments ultimately were dropped. But the plan being executed by Dunraven and his cohorts had been exposed.

Dunraven ultimately became weary of litigation, encroaching civilization and the feisty newcomers who were crowding his former hunting grounds. He never returned to Estes Park after the late 1880s, his wanderlust taking him to new adventures elsewhere in North America and abroad. Whyte departed for the British Isles in 1896. A few years after the turn of the century, Dunraven's holdings, including his remaining 6,400 acres of acquired land, were sold. The buyers: B.D. Sanborn, brother of C.W. Sanborn, the man who hired Alva Adams to work for his Greeley lumber business more than three decades earlier, and F.O. Stanley, whose grand hotel bearing his name remains an Estes Park landmark.

Dunraven's regular visits to Estes Park left behind lasting memories, but his legacy is not altogether lamented. In the words of author James H. Pickering, "The earl's ownership, which lasted until 1908, kept together in one piece large tracts of land, thus retarding the kind of unbridled development that would overtake Estes Park in the years that followed."[70]

Estes Valley pioneer Abner Sprague had offered the same opinion years earlier: "The holding of so much of the park by one company, even if it had been secured unlawfully, was the best thing for the place, particularly after it was proven that the place was only valuable because of its location and its attraction for lovers of the out-of-doors."[71]

Alex MacGregor, the man in the bowler hat near the center of the photo, added toll road builder and operator to his resume soon after moving to Estes Park. The road's opening in 1875 forever ended the valley's isolation. (Estes Park Area Historical Museum)

Chapter Seven

A Ranch and a Toll Road

*A*lex MacGregor, the newspaper editor from Wisconsin, became a jack of all trades in Colorado Territory. Western pioneers had to possess a number of skills to survive. They had to be inventive, to learn to make do.

When their 1875 diary commenced, Alex and Clara MacGregor resided at 351 Glenarm in Denver. Alex was a lawyer, with an office at the southeast corner of Holladay and 15th, but the home and office in Denver were temporary. Alex and Clara planned to move to Estes Park.

About two years earlier, MacGregor, envisioning life on a high country ranch, had searched for choice land, a place with not only water but timber, open fields and enough level land for pastures and crops. He found it, about a mile from what would become the thriving downtown of the resort community of Estes Park. Located immediately north of today's Elkhorn Avenue, the land boasted the most beautiful scenery the MacGregors had ever seen.

Alex, Clara and Georgianna Heeney also took advantage of the Homestead Act of 1862 in beginning their lives in the mountain valley. The homestead law allowed settlers, for a small fee, to obtain 160 acres provided they live on the land for five years, improve it and build a suitable house on the property. From the date of first application – or filing – six months were allowed for improvements; the claim cabin satisfied this requirement. If the settler had not abandoned the land for more than six months at any time, at the end of five years, he or she could prove up – or secure a final title to the land.

Using homestead rights and other legal methods of land acquisition, the MacGregors and Georgianna gained rights to hundreds of acres of high-country paradise. As the family established its holdings in Estes Park, Alex acted on his firm belief that a better road would encourage settlement. It had become evident that the beauty of the area would attract more and more permanent settlers, and tourists, as well.

Clara's mother was pleased with her son-in-law and his prospects for a successful future. Heeney also felt that the outlook for Colorado Territory was bright. Georgianna supported Alex's decision to build a toll road, and she contributed thousands of dollars to the funds he would need to open it.

MacGregor benefitted from a Colorado territorial statute encouraging private entrepreneurs to build wagon roads for public use. The statute required, among other things, that investors file articles of incorporation specifying the proposed road's termini and route. Upon complying with the statutory requirements, the investors gained a right of way over the intended route and at the completion of the road, they acquired the right to erect toll-gates and charge a toll, which could be regulated by local commissioners.

In September of 1874, MacGregor filed the articles of incorporation for the Park Road Company, listing as his associates Marshall Bradford and G. Heeney, his mother-in-law. The corporation's stated purpose was to construct and maintain a wagon road from the northern side of North St. Vrain Creek in Boulder County to Estes Park in Larimer County, and to collect tolls from persons traveling over the road.

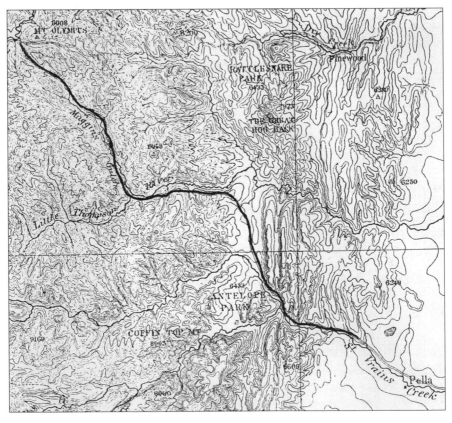

This old map shows the route followed by MacGregor's toll road. (Bill Van Horn)

The route MacGregor intended to carve out began near the Barney and Miller ranches on the North St. Vrain near present-day Lyons, heading generally northwest before crossing the Little Thompson River and traveling up Muggins Gulch. The toll road project, much of which followed near the course of today's U.S. 36 and ended at the MacGregors' Estes Park ranch, was an ambitious one. Alex began construction, hiring almost a dozen men during the time the road was built. Israel Rowe was MacGregor's assistant foreman, and his wife cooked for the road workers over an open fire while caring for the couple's two young children.

A new road through the area was badly needed. Prior to 1874, the only access to Estes Park was over pack horse trails or a crude cart road built by Joel Estes, the Estes Valley's first white settler and namesake, in the early 1860s. The condition of the old Estes road was accurately described by Hattie Carruthers, who took a trip by prairie schooner from Iowa to Estes Park in 1874: "The road was called a road only by courtesy. The rocks, streams and steep ascents made any trip to the Park something of an adventure." [72]

The year 1875 was a turbulent one for Alex and Clara. In January, their diary indicated that MacGregor's toll road workers were out of meat, one of his workmen had frozen both his ear and foot, MacGregor's horse had taken sick and died, and Clara was about to give birth to their first child. Alex was anxious to get back to his workmen, but because of his concern for Clara, he "could not go to Longmont or on the road."

Alex faithfully recorded the day-to-day occurrences in his journal:

Sunday, January 10 – Mare was taken sick in the night (4 a.m.). Went for horse doctor. After a search for an hour found Dr. Crane – Got Medicine of Parker & Linsley[73] – Mare was down – we could not [illegible word] her up. Dr. was up 3 or 4 times. Don't expect the horse to live until morning – said it was the Colic.

Monday, January 11 – Mare alive – Dr said he could save her – Had John Ring come up. Also hired Copeland (Reddy) to nurse her. At noon Dr. gave her another large Dose of Alloes, & from that time she was in convulsions until she died at 9:30 p.m. It was the 2d dose that killed her.

Tuesday, January 12 – Paid Thos Clarke $5.00 for burying mare. Reddy $2.00 to Druggist 6.85. I then found that the Dr. had got 1.50 of Brandy Charged to me which he drank – I therefore paid him only half of his bill 5.00 with his receipt in full. Colt doing finely.

The sick horse entry offered insights into how Alex thought. He felt it was fair to pay the veterinarian only half of what was due him because he had charged the brandy to Alex, and because drinking the brandy may have impaired his medical skills.

It also has been said that Alex paid more attention to his ailing horse than he did to Clara at the time of his child's birth. However, the subjects of pregnancy and childbirth, universal experiences, were seldom mentioned in letters and diaries of the time.[74]

The MacGregors' first son, George, was born in Denver on January 22, 1875, and Alex dutifully recorded the event.

Thursday, January 21 – Clara taken sick about midnight.

Friday, January 22 – Went for Dr. about 1:30 a.m. About 8:30 o'clock a.m., Clara bore unto me a son, 10 lb. clothes on. Clara doing finely.

Saturday, January 23 – Clara improving in health.

MacGregor left to go back to camp six days after George's birth while Georgianna remained with her daughter and the baby. The Denver trips took two or three days each way, and Alex saw his family infrequently. One day's ride from Denver, Longmont's St. Vrain Hotel, Griffith Evans, proprietor, often hosted the MacGregors on their trips to the plains.

Back at the ranch, Alex's men were helping him build three cabins: the MacGregors' claim cabin, another for Clara's mother and the third, perhaps, would be a bunkhouse. Several sources have suggested that Alex and Clara moved to their claim cabin in Estes Park in February of 1875, when their first son would have been only a month old. However, because the winter weather was severe only Alex and his workmen were in the area at that

Griff Evans' St. Vrain Hotel, located at the right portion of the photograph, was a regular Longmont stopover for the MacGregors. (Longmont Museum)

time. The tent they slept in blew down at least twice during rough weather. But despite the inclement conditions, the claim cabin was completed at about 4 p.m. on February 26, 1875, after its builders put on a pole and bough roof, added the door and window, and chinked the kitchen.

The baby was six weeks old and Alex was celebrating his 29th birthday when he next visited his family in Denver. The trip was difficult, with little or no sleep en route.

After MacGregor returned to his family on May 1, preparations began for the move to Estes Park. They left Denver with the baby and two wagons loaded with furniture on May 22. "A.Q. MacGregor and wife" and "L.A. Mills," one of Alex's earliest toll road workers and ranch hands and driver of the second team, were listed on the St. Vrain Hotel registry their first night out of Denver, giving their addresses as Estes Park. MacGregor recorded the journey in his diary:

Saturday, May 22, 1875 – Left Denver with Wife & Baby, 2 teams loaded with furniture for Estes Park.

Tuesday, May 25 – Nearly dead, am so tired.

Saturday, May 29 – Paid Walt Beach bal. on Bill of Lumber 10.50.

Monday, May 31 – Rec'd. of AQ MacGregor ($25.00) twenty-five dollars – the same being for wages on Estes Park Road. (Signed) John B. Reeder.

Wednesday, June 9 – Moved to the Park – stop in the Denison house. Fixed bridges around 7 mile hill. A horrable trip.

It took MacGregor 17 days to move his family to Estes Park. Oddly enough, given the length and difficulty of the trip itself, MacGregor made no other diary entries.

Alex left for Boulder and Longmont on business the day after the "horrable trip." Mills may have accompanied him as both men returned home on June 12.

Thursday, June 10 – Started for Boulder on Parker Winter matter with $13.00. Took John Dixons horse, went via Longmont. This money to Winters was Clara's.

Friday, June 11 – Wm. Higby – Boulder Horses shod.

Saturday, June 12 – Returned from Boulder via Longmont. Mother sick with Rheumatism. Mills brought siding.

A cabin built by Charles W. Denison in 1868 was the MacGregor family's temporary home upon its arrival in Estes Park in June of 1875. This outstanding two-story log structure located between the early cabins of

Built in 1868, the Denison cabin was the temporary home of the MacGregors when the family moved to Estes Park in 1875. (Denver Public Library)

Israel Rowe near Mt. Olympus and Griff Evans hosted the MacGregors until their own residences at the ranch were completed.

The Denison cabin was known as the Emmons Ranch House when the MacGregors moved in. "Paid Mrs. Emmons $5.00" was recorded on a memoranda page at the back of Alex's 1875 dairy, noting rent paid for June, 1875.

Horace Ferguson had brought his family to the Estes Park area two months before the MacGregors arrived. Ferguson found his land while on a hunting trip the previous winter and built a cabin about a half mile north of Marys Lake. He defied the Earl of Dunraven's claims by homesteading there, and later expanded his cabin into a summer resort hotel he called "The Highlands." Ferguson is credited with naming Bear Lake, a popular destination in today's Rocky Mountain National Park, after seeing a bear there.

The Ferguson and MacGregor families were frequent visitors at each other's homes. Alex surveyed land belonging to Ferguson's son, Hunter, in Willow Park, now Moraine Park, working with Hunter, Abner Sprague and Fred Sprague. All are remembered as important area pioneers.

Many persons came to the MacGregors' ranch to sketch views of the scenery, the barn or other features. The younger Ferguson daughters, Fanny (Frances) and Sally, often would spend the day at the ranch, possibly taking

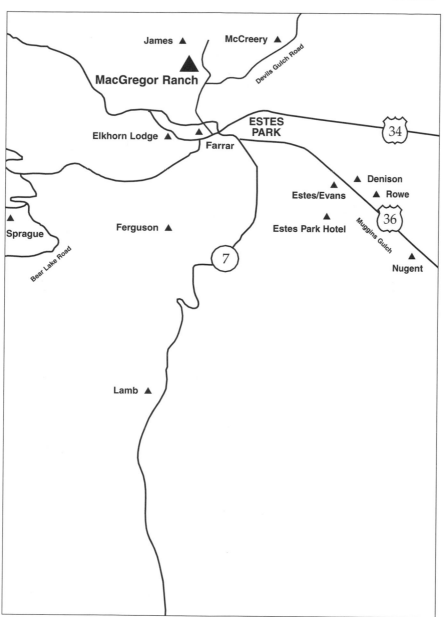

James ▲   McCreery ▲

Devils Gulch Road

MacGregor Ranch ▲

ESTES PARK

Elkhorn Lodge ▲   ▲
            Farrar

34

▲ Denison
Estes/Evans ▲   ▲ Rowe

36

Sprague ▲

Ferguson ▲

Estes Park Hotel ▲

Muggins Gulch

Bear Lake Road

7

Nugent ▲

Lamb ▲

THE HOMES
OF THE PIONEERS

art lessons from the talented Clara. Sally did considerable painting while visiting there, and Clara made out lists of paints that Sally might need.

In his diary entry of October 26, 1876, MacGregor noted that "Annee Ferguson married tonight a Mr. Hubbell (Uncle Dick)!" This was the first wedding to take place in Estes Park.

On occasion, Horace Ferguson furnished beef for the MacGregors:

Sunday, December 17, 1876 – Forrest (Hood) & Martie (McPherson) went over to Fergusons & got 100# Beef (hind qr. @ 8 cents). Beef very fine. Abner Sprague over.

Abner E. Sprague built his Moraine Park cabin in 1875. At age 25, he and his 16-year-old brother, Fred, developed their homestead in one of Colorado's more spectacular mountain valleys. Building a cabin from rough-hewn timber was one of their simpler challenges; furnishing it with "Carrie Nation furniture, made with a hatchet," as Sprague called it, seemed to be even less trouble. But Abner was struck down with a mysterious illness that kept him in bed for more than a month late that summer. And when Abner and Fred Sprague made the decision to remain in Moraine Park over the winter to watch their cattle herd, they were in for brutal weather.

Abner and Alberta Sprague were important figures in early Estes Park. (Photo courtesy of Edgar Stopher)

Abner, who had married Mary Alberta Morrison, whom he met while on a surveying job with the Missouri Pacific Railroad in Nebraska, soon found hosting visitors preferable to punching cattle. The Spragues took on a

The Spragues' property included this hotel. The resort, and all other structures developed there over the years, disappeared after Rocky Mountain National Park restored Moraine Park as a natural meadow. (Photo courtesy of Edgar Stopher)

partner, who later bought them out, and the homestead went on to became Stead's Ranch, a popular resort. After a few years, Abner and Alberta Sprague built a summer cottage in Glacier Basin and once again began entertaining visitors. Abner lived to age 93, and is credited with writing down much of the history of the Estes Park area.

Alex MacGregor relied heavily on a faithful associate, Henry "Hank" Farrar. A guide and hunter, Farrar also was known as "Buckskin." Farrar held the Joel Estes-Jacobs claim before Griff Evans controlled it and the land became lost in the domain of the Earl of Dunraven.

Farrar built his cabin about a mile south of the MacGregors, on land now part of downtown Estes Park. It also was property for which the English Company had received a patent granting title. Farrar was ordered to get out, or the company would put him out. His response was that he did not care to own the land and pay taxes on it as long as the company had to. He just wanted a place to live, and would remain until the company could prove that it had secured the land legally. As a compromise, the company deeded Farrar 80 acres just east of the property where the Elkhorn Lodge was later built by the James family, which homesteaded in Black Canyon on land adjacent to the MacGregors.

Entries in Alex and Clara's diaries hint of a problem between the James and MacGregor families. Alex built a fence between their properties, but the notations offer no explanation:

Monday, April 2, 1877 – James Moved today.

Thursday, April 5 – Fenced Today & finished around us far as James house. James set his barn on fire yesterday.

Friday, April 13 – In afternoon built fence in gap south of ranch – (between) self & James.

Eleanor E. Hondius, the only daughter of William E. and Ella McCabe James, suggested the reason for the antagonisms: "It was very difficult to determine legally what land was available since most of it was claimed by Lord Dunraven. Father took up a claim at the upper end of Black Canyon and built a cabin for his family there."

MacGregor's mother-in-law, Georgianna Heeney, also had filed a claim for the piece of land in question. The courts resolved the case in favor of Heeney. Time heals many wounds, and years later, Eleanor Hondius was gracious enough to make the statement that she would always be grateful

This wagon passed through the tollgate near today's Pinewood Springs in 1892. (Estes Park Area Historical Museum)

that her father got land where the Elkhorn Lodge now stands instead of his "jumped" claim. Otherwise, she'd "still be picking chokecherries at the upper end of Black Canyon."

None of these diversions would deter MacGregor from completing his road project. The July 28, 1875, diary notation announced, "Opened Road & commenced taking toll at noon." Alonzo "Lon" Parsons was the first gate-keeper for MacGregor's toll road, a route laboriously picked and shoveled out of the mountainous terrain. The tolls would be taken at various places over the years. The original tollgate was located where the road entered the foothills and later was moved to a place near the Little Thompson River known as Little Elk Park. At one time, the tollgate was situated near the Meining Ranch house in the vicinity of what is now Pinewood Springs.

Alex MacGregor's toll road ultimately would prove to be only a modest financial success. In time, it would become toll free and later, much of the old road would give way to a modern highway. But the Estes Valley now was open for business.

Then — as now — the view of the Estes Valley from Park Hill along the Lyons road was a dazzling sight to behold. (Denver Public Library)

Chapter Eight

CLARA AND ALEX IN ESTES PARK

*M*acGregor wasn't finished when the toll road was completed. He had big plans for the land he occupied in Estes Park.

On October 24, 1876, Alexander commented in the MacGregor diary, "Sawed today." The MacGregor sawmill operation clearly was the culmination of many months of active preparation. The mill was operated by streamwater dropping 30 feet upon a Leffel wheel and producing 18 horsepower. It was very important to the Estes Park community. In the words of Abner Sprague:

> *Mr. MacGregor put in a small sawmill in 1876, power generated by water through a turbine by water taken from the Black Canyon creek. This mill was a great help to all the settlers, as well as to MacGregor. Timber could be cut from their lands or from any public lands, the logs hauled to the mill, where Mr. MacGregor would saw it into lumber, taking toll for his work; no cash being required in the transaction. Only for this small mill, building material would have had to be hauled from the valley or the mills in the foothills, which would have cost more money and labor than most of the pioneers could have afforded at that time.*[75]

One of the buildings on the MacGregors' Black Canyon ranch housed Estes Park's first post office. Clara was the valley's first postmaster. This same structure was the site of a store where she sold many goods, including vegetables she had raised such as peas, lettuce and potatoes, as well as dairy products and other items and sundries. Clara juggled her tasks of caring for her son, milking the cows, cooking, assisting Alex with the management of the ranch, dispensing stamps or sending registered letters at the post office, and selling everything from bacon, fat pork, flour and corn meal to candles, kerosene and an occasional calico dress at the store. As late as September 22, 1882, Clara wrote that the Theodore Whytes paid her $10 to use a milk cow for the summer to feed their baby. She must have kept art supplies to sketch landscapes during her rare spare moments. Among the newspaper clippings Clara saved in her scrapbook were several praising her artistic ability. Appearing on page three:

Clara's painting of the ranch sawmill. (MacGregor Ranch)

One of the attractions of the MacGregor house is a collection of oil paintings, the work of Mrs. MacGregor, a pupil of Prof. Ford of Chicago. Among the number there are several of especial beauty and merit: "Sunset on the Platte," "Mt. Yale, Head of the Arkansas," "Garden of the Gods," and the "Coming Storm," are particularly worthy of note. The presence of such excellent works of art in this far off retreat occasion pleasure and surprise.

Trading work, bartering and borrowing helped the pioneers through the toughest days when money was in short supply. The MacGregors often accepted other items than cash for purchases at their store. At the sawmill, they took various goods or services in exchange for lumber or for sawing logs. Alex recorded many of these exchanges in his diary:

Monday, June 14, 1875 – Traded Red ox to Mr. Barber for 12 acres of plowing.

Friday, November 24 – Sprague over and said I could take pay for sawing logs out of 10 & 12 ft logs. He wanted the 16 ft Logs.

Saturday, December 23 – Arrangement with Wyman, he to have Allie & Ginger & wagon & to give me 400# of meat at 3 cents & get Ginger Shod & be back Tuesday week.

Friday, January 26, 1877 – Traded Nettie (Clara added, "my riding pony") to Lon Parsons for yoke of Cattle (one Bull 4 years old – 1 stag 3 years old – yoke – chain & whip) and Seven 50/100 Cash.

Wednesday, February 21 – Settled with Nate Runnels. He owes $12.20 to this date and from this on his rate of toll is to be 50 cents & the same as cash at the Gate. That is, I take lumber at 16$ per m (thousand feet) at the gate. He to have lumber at all times at gate to pay for his Toll and not to owe for Toll.

Tuesday, April 17 – Settled up with (Isaac H.) Hildreth tonight & I owe him for hay & work $148.27. He wants it by last of May. He says he is going to bring over a sack of Potatoes in Ex. for Cabbage Plants.

Over the years, Alex and Clara built three ranch homes on their successful hay and cattle spread. The first house was constructed in 1875, the second, an extension of an original homestead cabin, was completed in 1882. Their final home was begun in 1896. They also ran the post office, general store and welcomed tourists.

Newspaper correspondents filed many stories about the newly developing summer resort of Estes Park, and the early days of the MacGregors' ranch. The following undated clippings from unidentified sources who misspelled the family name were estimated to have been written around 1877, and are among the many newspaper articles preserved within Clara's scrapbook.

The view of Longs Peak from Mr. MacGregor's residence is indescribably grand. . . . Culture and refinement are far from strangers to the Park. The hum of the sewing machine and the silvery notes of the piano are heard here, under the shadow of the snowy peaks; and the walls of Mr. MacGregor's house are adorned with paintings – the work of Mrs. MacGregor – which would rank among the best. A natural artist, this lady finds in a wondrous mountain retreat much to satisfy a cultured and innate love of the sublime and the beautiful.

McGregor's (is) a pretty romantic spot where one can find "Rest for the weary soul" in a fine piano perfectly tuned, a guitar, violin, chest of Homeopathic medicines, arm chairs and other luxuries of civilization. Near McGregor's, above the sawmill, are quite a field of campers. Parties from St. Louis, Chicago, Omaha, Denver and Boulder attracted by shade and water form a striking mosaic of camps.

The second article read: *A.Q. McGregor, who has been spoken of as possessing a neat home in Black Canyon, has, besides the house in which his family lives, cottages with rooms sufficient to accommodate about thirty different guests.*

This is one of the pleasant little homes of the country. Its walls hang with paintings of rare merit, all the work of Mrs. McGregor, an artist and a real lady whom it does one good to meet. Her especial delight as an artist is tree painting, and her birch, beech and oak trees are well executed. A very sweet toned piano is also in this house where the guest who enjoys the sweet sounds may have them to his heart's content.

Mr. McGregor has a well-assorted little stock of camp supplies, fishing tackle, tobacco, cigars, groceries, canned goods, etc. His supply of trout flies and fishing tackle will be complete and the very best the market can afford. One Mr. Hildreth has perfected arrangements to run a hack and keep a number of ponies for the accommodation of guests. He will be stationed at the McGregor House, as this little home is called. Mr. McGregor has a small water power saw-mill with which he saws the timber used in

Life on the MacGregors' ranch in Black Canyon was decidedly slow paced in the 1870s. (Denver Public Library)

constructing his cottages, and just now he is engaged in building a large barn the timbers for which he is sawing himself.

The newspaper clippings in Clara's scrapbook describing the MacGregors' resort do not furnish a clue about the relationship between "Mr. Hildreth" and Alex. From the diaries, we learn that Alex's ranch hand, Isaac Howell Hildreth, performed almost every imaginable task on the ranch. And when Hildreth requested time off to work on his own house, Alex almost always agreed. But from time to time, Hildreth had differences with MacGregor, quitting numerous times and then returning, always to be welcomed back.

As the ranch was expanding, the community grew. The Estes Park census in 1880 reveals much about the activities in the new village. The census taker listed 171 residents in 39 dwellings. Occupants were farmers, laborers, stockmen, dairymen, loggers, sawyers, engineers, miners, teamsters and carpenters. There were two blacksmiths, a merchant, a liveryman, a stableman, a cow herder, a hotel manager, a hotel clerk and a bank bookkeeper.

Horace Ferguson kept boarders and Elkanah Lamb was a clergyman. One of Theodore Whyte's three servants was a cook from Prussia and John Cleave from England, well known for his carpentry, boarded at the Whytes. L.A. White's household included three lodgers – two carpenters and a miner. There was a visitor from Wisconsin at the MacGregor residence, and at the same dwelling lived one of the village's two mothers-in-law, Clara's mother, Georgianna Heeney, who no doubt also was helpful with the little boys, George, 5, and Donald, 2.

Daughters' occupations were invariably listed on the census report as "at home" from age 10 through their 20s. Without exception, the 30 persons whose relationship to the head of the family was listed as "wife" had their occupations described as "keeping house." Living on the frontier would have been at best difficult without a helpmate. Survival in the wilds was a full-time business.

In the following passage referring to his boyhood in Wisconsin, Alva Adams expressed the nature of frontier ranch life:

> *Soap was home-made. Our meat was grown in our own pasture or pen, with the addition of deer, quail, prairie chicken, pheasant, squirrel, rabbit and pigeon. Our blankets were woven by our grandmother from the wool of our own sheep. The spinning wheel held the place of honor where the Victrola stands now.*
>
> *To have bought eggs, butter or cheese would have seemed criminal extravagance. . . . Bedsteads were oak, walnut or mahogany that had come from our ancestry. They were corded and featherbeds were universal. On the cords was a straw-tick and on that a featherbed. In summer these beds were as comfortable as the beds of spikes affected by religious fakirs in India. I held to the featherbed until married, when it was made into pillows.[76]*

Planting and tending a vegetable garden was another household chore usually left to the woman of the house. And growing vegetables was no easy feat in the cold and wind common at the MacGregors' high-altitude spread. Not only was the weather hard on the plants outdoors, but the diary entry on April 29, 1877, noted that the 11 below zero temperature "half an hour after sunrise" caused some of Clara's houseplants inside the house to freeze.

Frontier women were hard working and inventive. In the words of one western historian, "Making clothing for herself and other members of the family was one of the most time-consuming household tasks for a woman. Earlier arrivals cut up their tents and wagon covers to make coats, and used remnants of old woolen garments to line them. Buttons could be cast of pewter by cutting molds from blocks of soapstone. Some emigrants brought their wool cards and spinning wheels from the East so they might spin yarn to make winter underclothing and stockings."[77]

Wash day meant Monday and Tuesday; the term should have been "wash days." In the earliest days, there was no bar soap. Soft soap and hot water were put into a keg and the clothes were dumped into the mixture. The clothes were vigorously prodded with a stick, then taken out and laid on a block and pounded with a mallet.

The MacGregor family at home in Estes Park (from left): Clara, Halbert, Donald, Alex and George. (MacGregor Ranch)

When the clothes were sufficiently clean, they were hung on bushes or fences to dry. Washboards, boilers and machines were unheard of. Frequently, the women migrated to a little creek or branch on wash day. The 10-gallon iron kettle and the clothes were taken to the bank of the stream and there, where wood and water were plentiful, the washing was done and the clothes hung out to dry. Afterward, the big kettle was turned upside down and left there as the dry clothes were taken to the house.[78]

Wash days were labor intensive in the high country, but mountain women enjoyed certain advantages over their plains counterparts. The Denver City Water Company began pumping water for residences in Colorado's capital city as early as 1872. However, the water piped from the South Platte River near its confluence with Cherry Creek was polluted. According to one account, "Housewives fitted their faucets with strainers to catch the small fish that came squirming through, but strainers did not filter out germs." People were advised to buy water from the mountains.[79]

MOVING ON

*A*lex and Clara were to have three sons. Their second boy, Donald, was born on February 11, 1878. It is believed that Clara was in Denver at the time of his birth, as well as for the birth of their third son, Halbert, born November 6, 1887.[80]

Donald would have been a year old and George 4 when the *Rocky Mountain News* announced on September 14, 1879, that Clara was back at her studio, enjoying marked success.

For at least several years, the MacGregors maintained two homes in Colorado. In the early months of 1882, they apparently decided to make the ranch in Estes Park their summer home and reside in Denver the remainder of the year. George was 7 years old that January, and it was time for him to begin school. The MacGregors may have felt the Denver school superior to the one that had opened in Estes Park the year before.

Health might have been another factor prompting the MacGregors to choose the city over more difficult ranch life, especially in winter. But as long as the MacGregors owned the toll road, it needed overseeing, and as long as Clara and Alex lived, they never lost their heartfelt interest in the ranch.

Perhaps the decision to winter in Denver was made, in part, because the MacGregors hoped to further Alex's legal career or Clara's art pursuits. There certainly were new developments in the field of art in Denver at that time. An announcement was made in the August 13, 1882, *Denver Tribune* regarding the city's emerging Academy of Fine Arts:

The artists of Denver acting together have secured the entire 5th floor of the Tabor Grand Opera House Bldg., and will occupy it at once. This fact will be received with joy by all admirers of art in its different branches and will open the eyes of the outside world as to Denver's taste and culture. . . . A beginning has been made in fitting up the exhibition room and school room for drawing classes in the Academy of Fine Arts on the corner of the Tabor Grand. Now the artists are moving to put the whole floor, some twenty-eight rooms and pairs of suites, to studio purposes.

Charles Partridge Adams, whose painting hangs in the home on the ranch today, was a charter member of the Denver Artists' Club, which in 1893 would become the Denver Art Museum. Also preserved at the ranch are an oil painting by Henry Crawford Ford and two of Helen Chain's paintings: an oil painting of the Mount of the Holy Cross and another mountain scene in watercolor.

Beginning in early 1882, Alex and Clara rented their ranch house to a Mr. McCabe for five years. On February 9, they moved into the cabin so McCabe could occupy their house. Two weeks later, the MacGregors left Estes Park for Denver, where they set up residence at 612 California St. But they returned to Estes Park for the summer in mid-April of 1882.

The MacGregors' plans were altered when on May 20, 1882, Alex was appointed to the bench in Larimer County (Fort Collins) following Judge T.M. Robinson's resignation. In November, 1882, MacGregor was elected to serve out the remainder of the unexpired term. He commuted between Fort Collins and Estes Park in the summer of 1882 while his family remained in the park. The home now known as the "A.Q. House" at the ranch was in the process of being expanded from a homestead cabin into a larger frame house with lath and plaster walls. In October, the family made another move, this time to Fort Collins.[81]

Alva Adams and his family also made a number of moves during the 1870s and early 1880s as Adams extended his businesses into southwestern Colorado. The Adams lived in South Pueblo in 1873 and 1876; Del Norte, 1875; Garland City, 1877; Alamosa, 1878; and South Pueblo, 1882. In the spring of 1883, for business and perhaps political reasons, the Adams decided to make Pueblo their permanent home.

The MacGregor and Adams families remained acquaintances over the years. In 1882, Alva gave Alex and Clara a stained-glass door for their newly remodeled home, the A.Q. House. The ranch still possesses the book *The Story of a Bad Boy* by Thomas Bailey Aldrich, which 10-year-old Donald received as a gift with the inscription "Donald MacGregor from Alva Adams, 1888." Ella and Alva's young son, Alva Blanchard Adams, was just three years older than Donald and the same age as George.

Alex's bid for reelection to the bench in November of 1884 was unsuccessful. His term ended the following January, and he opened a law practice in Fort Collins. That fall, the family moved again, making Highlands, near Denver, its home. Alva Adams also was defeated at the polls in 1884, having been nominated to run for governor for the first time.

Alva sent the following note to Clara concerning his unsuccessful try for the office. The letterhead was that of "Alva Adams & A.D. Craigue, Hardware Merchants, South Pueblo," and was dated Nov. 8, 188 – (1884). The "Blaine" mentioned by Alva in his letter was James Gillespie Blaine, a United States congressman from Maine. Speaker of the House in 1875 when the Colorado statehood measure was introduced, Blaine had been instrumental in its passage.

South Pueblo, Colo.
Nov. 8, 188

   Dear Clara,

   The war is over and I am not one of the victors. There are too many Blaine men in Colo. – I am proud of the race I made as I ran ahead of my ticket everywhere but there was too large a majority to overcome – Larimer Co & Ft Collins performed more than their duty. All things considered that county treated me as well or better than any other co – I am glad the fight is over and I have no regrets over the result. While I would have been glad to have been elected I realize that it is better for me that I can now attend to my own affairs and that affords some consolation – my friends regret my defeat more than I.

   Hope your health is better and that your visit will be full of pleasure – Hope to see you return home as healthy & happy as the girl I used to know.

   Weather has been perfect all the fall and that has been a partial recompense for the dull times that have prevailed – now that Cleveland is elected I hope for better days.

   As Ever Yours,
   Alva A

Governor Alva Adams.
(Denver Public Library)

In November of 1886, just 15 years from the time Alva Adams brought his mother and the five younger children to Colorado by covered wagon and hauled ties for the railroad, he was elected governor of Colorado. In a state normally Republican, this was quite a feat for a Democrat. Adams also was recognized as Colorado's youngest governor and the first businessman to hold the position. After serving his two-year term, he returned to his business in Pueblo until 1896, when he was elected Colorado's chief executive for a second term.

Adams would be elected a third time in 1904, but his residence in the governor's mansion would be short lived. After serving three months of his term, Alva was unseated by the Republican majority, culminating rancor between the two political parties over alleged election rigging. Adams left office despite the fact that most evidence cleared him of any wrongdoing, according to press reports.

Despite the scandal, Adams' reputation remains intact. One biographer described him in these words: "The keynote of Alva Adams' character throughout has been – purpose. . . . What he is he has made himself, and my heart goes out in unreserved sympathy toward the high and honorable and forcible character he has established." [82]

While the rest of Alva Adams' life was carefully documented, "Knowledge of the remaining years of Alexander and Clara MacGregor's lives is sketchy at best," according to one biographical publication. "They continued to take a vital interest in their Estes Park ranch, buying and selling land, and leasing cabins. Most likely they continued to summer on the ranch.[83] On March 31, 1891, Clara lost her mother, Georgianna, age 63.

At the time of a land purchase in January, 1894, the MacGregors were residents of Arapahoe County. Sometime during that year, they must have moved back to Estes Park. On January 16, 1895, A.Q. MacGregor was sworn in as justice of the peace for Estes Park, precinct number 20. He served in that capacity for the year and was sworn in again on Dec. 3, 1895.[84] In April of 1896, Alex and Clara took a memorable trip to Alaska, throughout their journey sending detailed reports of their travels to their sons. Also in the early months of 1896, construction was begun on a larger ranch home for the MacGregor family.

But tragedy would prevent Alex MacGregor from moving into the home MacGregor Ranch visitors enjoy today.

Chapter Ten

ALEX'S DEATH AND
CLARA'S LIFE AFTERWARD

*B*efore construction of the third house on the MacGregor Ranch could be completed, Alex was killed by a lightning strike high in the nearby mountains. The date was June 17, 1896.

It was not generally known that in addition to Alex's other interests, he and son George shared a passion for mining.[85] Alexander MacGregor died at age 50, while he and his oldest son were doing assessment work on a mining claim.

The Monday morning *Denver Republican* of June 22, 1896, reported the incident that dealt a stunning blow to the Estes Park pioneer family. Alex and his eldest son were:

. . . .prospecting above timberline, on a spur of the Continental Divide at the headwaters of the Big Thompson and Grand river, fifteen miles from help or habitation. Both were prostrated by a flash from a sudden electrical storm. When the son recovered consciousness, his father was dead. Finding he could do nothing for his father in his lame and dazed condition, he crawled to his pony and went for assistance. . . . A relief party of six men was soon formed, returned after twelve hours with their burden.

Clara was in Denver at the time and her second son, Donald, who was at the ranch when the accident occurred, brought the bad news to his mother. She was left alone with their three sons, George, age 21, Donald, 18, and Halbert, not yet 9. Clara had the original five rooms of the planned ranch house completed, but leased the ranch to the Johnson brothers and moved to Denver. According to ranch history, Clara had offered the ranch for sale at least once, changing her mind before any offer was accepted.

Two and a half years after the lightning strike killed Alex, Clara and Alva still were keeping their families in touch, as is evident in this letter from Alva written while he was serving as governor:

Dec. 25, 1898
State of Colorado
Executive Chamber
Denver

Dear Clara,

I thank you for your Christmas token. I hope you are happy and content this holiday season — I have not time even to think whether I am happy or not — As Myron Reed said, I am as busy as a train dispatcher. I have one satisfaction and that is that a day of rest is near. I hope we will enjoy it as much as expected. We will go to Pasadena for a month and then home and at work — Mother had a fall and hurt her arm and shoulder and is laid up — I wish the folks lived in Colorado so we might be near them — Cali is so far away.

With all of the good wishes of the day.

Sincerely,
Alva Adams

Alva's parents moved to California in 1890 and celebrated their golden wedding anniversary in December, 1897. When the Adams came to Denver from Pasadena to visit Alva for several months in January of 1898, their daughter, Libbie Adams, accompanied them.

John Adams died in Pasadena in 1908. His wife, Eliza, passed away three years later. Libbie would live until 1929, dying at age 70 while her brother, William H. Adams, was serving as Colorado's governor. Libbie outlived her brother, Alva, and in her last years she made her home with Alva's widow, Ella, and her only other surviving brother, John Adams Jr.

Clara Heeney MacGregor, country girl turned artist, pioneer settler, wife, mother, ranch operator and successful businesswoman, died in Denver in 1901. Alex, Clara and Clara's mother, Georgianna, all are buried in that city's Riverside Cemetery. The final letter from Alva preserved by Clara bore the postmark "Madison, Wisconsin, June 15, 1900." It was addressed "2816 W. 25th St., Denver, Colo."

Madison, June 15

Dear Clara,

Your letter reached me here where we are to visit a few days. Your note is home but I will send it when I get back and you can regard it as cancelled & should a cyclone strike me this will be your receipt in full. I return the interest check as you have paid enough.

We visit Blanchardville and I will also go to the woods in north Wisc. for a week or so.

Expect to be home in three weeks.

Sincerely,
Alva Adams

It appears that Alva had loaned Clara a sum of money, for what purpose we may never know. Perhaps the funds paid expenses of the boys' educations or covered expenditures of the MacGregor home or the ranch. Alva's loan might have helped Clara make one of her land purchases after Alex's death. Or, it is conceivable that Clara may have had excessive medical expenses. Alva's letter canceling the remainder of the debt came less than a year before Clara's death at age 48.

Alva Adams, the man who brought his family to the new frontier in covered wagons and went on to lead Colorado through early statehood, died in Battle Creek, Michigan, on November 1, 1922, of diabetes and heart complications. He was survived by his widow, Ella; son, Alva B., one of the leading attorneys of Pueblo (not yet a U.S. senator); three brothers: Senator William H. Adams, acknowledged Democratic leader in the Colorado Legislature (not yet governor of Colorado), Frank Adams, president of Colorado Ice and Cold Storage Company of Denver, and John Adams, a stockman in Alamosa County, Colorado.

Alva Adams died in 1922. His political legacy lived on. (Colorado Historical Society)

In his eulogy, Alva's friend, J.F. Keating, paid tribute to the role of the frontier in the life of Alva Adams:

In the environment of the frontier, he developed his manhood, as in an earlier day did the great Lincoln. In that environment he found as associates all sorts and conditions of men; the coarse, the carefree, even the criminal, as well as an occasional man of the nobler and better kind. Yet this sort of environment, that destroyed so many, was through the sheer force of their wills and their faiths and the qualities of their natures, made to mould a Lincoln and an Adams.[86]

Relatively pristine, unspoiled and remarkably scenic, Rocky Mountain National Park hosts millions of visitors each year. (David Halpern)

Chapter Eleven

ROCKY MOUNTAIN NATIONAL PARK

*T*he generation of Americans that witnessed the closing of the frontier also created a system of national parks, national forests and state forests for public use and enjoyment and preservation of the dwindling wilderness. Rocky Mountain National Park became the 10th national park established by Congress when it opened on September 15, 1915.

In 1907, about the time Donald MacGregor took over the ranch operations, Enos Abijah Mills promoted the idea of creating a large national park near Estes Park. The persistent lobbying efforts of this celebrated writer, naturalist, mountain guide and innkeeper proved to be a major – if not decisive – factor in the creation of the park.[87]

Mills (1870-1922) bought the Longs Peak Inn from Reverend Elkanah Lamb's son, Carlyle, in 1902, and rebuilt it in 1906 after it had burned. Demonstrating his interest in trees, he used "fire-killed trunks and branches as screens, spindles for staircases and porch railings. This rustic architecture was an unfailing conversation piece, Mills always turning the conversation into a nature lesson," according to one account.[88]

Mills spoke not only for the trees, but "also for the animals, the rivers and the mountains," another historian wrote. "No matter how often he was ignored or ridiculed, he spoke out – to citizens, congressmen and presidents – about the importance of national parks."[89]

While it is tempting to downplay his role – many other individuals and organizations were involved – the part Mills played was both dominant and critical. During a few short years, he wrote more than 2,000 letters, penned 64 newspaper and magazine articles, distributed 430 photographs and gave 42 lectures promoting the park concept.[90] Mills today is remembered as the "father of Rocky Mountain National Park."

James Grafton Rogers also is widely credited for his efforts in the establishment of Rocky Mountain National Park. Rogers, who served with the State Department in Washington and worked as a Denver attorney and law school dean, was one of the founders and the first president of the Colorado Mountain Club, which was organized to protect the national park.[91] The for-

Enos Mills (left) and F.O. Stanley (second from left) celebrated the opening of Rocky Mountain National Park in 1915. (Denver Public Library)

mation of the Estes Park Protective and Improvement Association in September, 1906, also marked a milestone in efforts to promote preservation of the local natural scene.

Other individuals mentioned as deserving a share of the credit for the creation of Rocky Mountain National Park include H.N. Wheeler, F.O. Stanley, Cornelius Bond and a number of other dedicated people. The park would assure that at least a portion of the Colorado Rockies forever would serve as a reminder of what the pioneers found. In one book's words:

When the park was established, the region was still primarily wilderness, home to the mountain lion and the grizzly bear, much of it untrammeled by people but for the occasional Ute or trapper hardy enough to have roamed its ridges. Yet Enos Mills knew that time was fast running out. More and more settlers were streaming westward. Local elk had already been hunted almost to extinction. . . .

Nearly a century later, Rocky Mountain National Park exists in close proximity to four million people, little more than an hour's drive from metropolitan Denver. Last year, more than three million people visited the park, about the same number who visited Yellowstone, a park eight times the size. The elk population has rebounded to a number that creates management problems outside the park and devastation of willow and aspen groves inside. The towns of Estes Park and Grand Lake, hugging tight to the park's boundaries, continue to expand.[92]

Today, MacGregor Ranch and Rocky Mountain National Park are an island of preservation amid a sea of change.

(Clockwise from top left) Minnie Maude MacGregor, Donald MacGregor and their daughter, Muriel, whose wishes were honored by the ranch's preservation. (MacGregor Ranch)

Chapter Twelve

THE END OF THE RAINBOW

*H*igh in the Rocky Mountains of Colorado, near the famed resort community of Estes Park, lies the picturesque MacGregor Ranch. The ranch sits in a snug valley, on a slope facing Longs Peak. It is shielded from much of the area's urban development by sharp contours of the land. The northern boundaries of the MacGregor Ranch adjoin Rocky Mountain National Park at the end of MacGregor Avenue. Just above the ranch property line, a parking lot is provided for a trailhead offering access to the Lumpy Ridge area in the popular park.[93]

Alex and Clara MacGregor's middle son, Donald, took over some of the management of the family holdings, perhaps even before the death of his father. A pricing agent for a machinery distributor called the Hendrie-Bolthoff Manufacturing & Supply Company, he married Minnie Maude Koontz, whose family also had come to Colorado from Wisconsin. Donald and Maude's only child, Muriel, was born in Denver on April 2, 1904, eight years after her grandfather's death in 1896 and three years after her grandmother died.

Realizing that he wanted to continue the ranching traditions begun by his father, Donald bought out the ranch interests of his brothers and moved his family from Denver to the ranch in 1907, when Muriel was 3.

Donald MacGregor increased the size of the ranch to more than 3,000 acres during his years of operation, also changing from raising polled hereford cattle to the more profitable black angus stock. Donald MacGregor enlarged the five-room house that had been intended for Alex and Clara's final home. The stained-glass door from the A.Q. House given to Alexander and Clara by Alva was moved to grace the entrance of the residence Alex did not live to see completed. The Donald MacGregors lived in this expanded third ranch house, which today serves as a museum.

Alex and Clara MacGregor's oldest son, George, graduated from the Colorado School of Mines with an engineering degree in June of 1897, one year after witnessing his father's death. George seemed to want nothing to do with the ranch after the horrifying experience. However, at age 65, his

MacGregor Ranch hands brand cattle in the early 1900s. (Piet Hondius)

dreams once again turned to ranching. In 1940, he was running a 160-acre ranch and raising 30 head of Guernsey cattle near Terrebonne, Oregon.

Alex and Clara's youngest son, Halbert, was a witness at Donald's marriage to Maude, and he did visit the ranch on occasion through the years. In 1912, Halbert received a bachelor of science degree in chemical engineering from the University of Illinois, traveling extensively while working in that field. He served as a consultant and represented corporations in court cases.

Donald and Maude's daughter, Muriel, was a shy child who loved her life on the ranch. At age 6, she rode her pony to school when she began her education in Estes Park. Muriel became an accomplished rider and from an early age on, she helped her parents with the chores about the ranch. Muriel also enjoyed writing, and spent quite a bit of time composing notes to send to her "aunties" while she was visiting with her mother in the kitchen.

Muriel spent her entire life on the ranch, except when she was away at school. In 1921, after 11 years in the Estes Park schools and one year before she would have graduated from high school, she was accepted as a student at The Colorado College in Colorado Springs. She received a bachelor of arts degree from the college in June, 1925, a master of arts degree from the University of Colorado in June of 1931 and a law degree from the University of Denver in June, 1934. In 1936, Muriel MacGregor became one of the two women admitted that year to practice law before the Colorado Supreme Court.

Although a lawyer, she spent much of her time helping her father on the ranch, also writing short stories and composing music. Her law practice was limited to filing collection suits for the business analyst firm of Dunn and Bradstreet, administering estates and handling other minor legal matters for local Estes Park residents.

Muriel never was encouraged to date. If a ranch hand showed too much interest in her, he received his severance pay at his breakfast plate. She never married, and was the last MacGregor to live on the ranch property. After losing both of her parents in 1950, she lived alone for 20 years. Despite her heroic efforts to keep the ranch intact and in repair, Muriel was plagued by debts and failing health. It was difficult to make ends meet – much less make a profit – raising cattle at an altitude ranging from 7,600 to 9,000 feet.

With considerable effort, and by selling some of her land, Muriel held the ranch together until her death in 1970 at the age of 66. Her will specified that the ranch and cattle herd be preserved and maintained insofar as possible, and that the net proceeds from the production of the ranch and its cattle herd be used for charitable and educational purposes. The provisions of Muriel's three-page will spawned more than a decade of legal wrangling and estate erosion.

While the MacGregors had accumulated considerable land, there was inadequate capital to handle the ranch's operation during the final period of family ownership. The MacGregor case was a textbook example of being "land poor." The land was worth millions, but there was no cash to satisfy the estate's debts, even before death taxes were considered. It has been claimed that poverty is a friend of preservation. Because of the lack of adequate funds, there was no extensive remodeling on the ranch during the MacGregors' lifetimes, As a result, the ranch remains almost exactly as it was during the MacGregor era.

On September 4, 1976, a retired veterinarian and MacGregor Ranch volunteer, Dr. Benjamin F. Stearn, sent a letter to James Riley, assistant attorney general for the State of Colorado, requesting a meeting to discuss ranch problems. Ruth Ann Gartland of the attorney general's office met with a group of staunch volunteers at the Stearn home to discuss possible means of preserving the ranch. As a result of this conversation, Riley and Howard Kenison, also of the attorney general's office, were assigned to work on the ranch project. Over a long period of time, and after a series of complicated legal steps had been taken, a satisfactory solution was finally reached.

To satisfy debts that had accumulated during Muriel MacGregor's lifetime and pay estate taxes, the trustees of her estate planned to sell off a portion of the land to raise funds. However, the state attorney general's office prohibited the sale of any land for payment of debts or death taxes.

The first step in saving the MacGregor Ranch from the developers' bulldozers was this landmark sale-blocking decision by the attorney general's office. Eldon Freudenburg, chairman of the board of trustees for the MacGregor Trust, lauded Riley and Kenison for their perseverance in preventing sale of the property to private interests. "The real treasure is that the ranch has been saved for posterity," Freudenburg said.

In Washington, Representative Hank Brown (R-Colo.) and Senator Bill Armstrong (R-Colo.) spearheaded a congressional battle to raise funds to secure a conservation easement that would bring the ranch under Rocky Mountain National Park's protective umbrella. In a last-ditch effort, Brown played a key role in attaching the funds to the supplemental appropriations bill, beating a deadline that had been imposed by Congress.

Armstrong provided an influential voice in helping the MacGregor package pass through the Senate's Appropriations subcommittee, which had rejected the plan the previous year. James Johnson, a former member of Colorado's congressional delegation and now a MacGregor Ranch trustee, provided great assistance in this effort.

Most of the legal disputes were resolved in 1983, when the National Park Service agreed to the terms of a $4-million conservation easement. Thirteen years after her death, Muriel MacGregor's bequest was finally honored. While the MacGregor Ranch is located within the boundaries of

Alex MacGregor didn't live to see the completion of the house that today serves as a museum at his Estes Park ranch. (John Gunn)

Rocky Mountain National Park, the Muriel L. MacGregor Charitable Trust is its owner. The easement permits the continuation of ranching operations, but bars any commercial development. The trustees' policy of operating on interest generated by the Park Service payment assures that the ranch will enter the future true to Muriel's charitable and educational dictates.

For James Godbolt, acting superintendent of Rocky Mountain National Park at the time of the agreement, the release of the MacGregor funds was welcome news. Chester Brooks, who retired from the top park post a few months earlier, had set as one of his final goals the acquisition of a conservation easement to preserve the historical site. The easement goal was included in the park's master plan, and was pursued doggedly throughout Brooks' tenure. His sentiments were almost universal. Dr. William Morgan, chairman of the MacGregor Ranch trustees at the time of the settlement, described the ranch as a unique and irreplaceable example of early homestead pioneer development of mountain cattle ranches along the Front Range.

Also assisting the ranch preservation was Pieter Hondius, then president-elect of the Colorado Mountain Club, who helped coordinate a grassroots lobbying effort to gain congressional approval for the funds. Hondius credited "hundreds of people who worked so hard" for the release of the MacGregor funds, citing letters of endorsement from the Estes Park Board of Trustees, Larimer County Board of Commissioners and the Estes Park Area Chamber of Commerce.

A *Denver Post* newspaper article also celebrated this victory by the forces of preservation:

There is sweet reward when you look back at something that was a bitter, bitter battle for more than 13 years, and The Good Guys not only won, but another decade later, the benefits to the state and its people still multiply. That's the tale of the historic MacGregor Ranch, owned by one family from 1873 until the last descendant, Muriel, age 66, died in 1970. The rapid development of the town at that time almost destroyed the ranch next to Rocky Mountain National Park — but didn't because of a hardy band of backers who fought to maintain the ranch as a historic resource.

Today the MacGregor Ranch is exactly that, an absolutely irreplaceable house museum, filled with all the belongings of one country family for almost a century, and the ranch buildings and land as an invaluable record of a pioneer mountain ranch. A visitor might think the family was all out doing the chores, for there are clothes in the closet, dishes on the table, treasured items about.[94]

At this writing, the 1,200-acre ranch maintains three bulls and approximately 65 cows and their calves. Outlying pastures at Dry Gulch, Elk Pasture and Piper Meadow account for an additional 542 acres. Care of the hay and cattle ranch is not a simple task. While full ranch operations continue, management is also concerned with the care of its museum-designated buildings. The ranch's inclusion in the National Register of Historic Places listed 41 buildings on the property, 28 of which were judged to be contributing to the MacGregor Ranch historic district. The earliest of these buildings were constructed in the 1870s, and all of the contributing buildings were erected before 1939.

Paramount in the trustees' agenda has been its determination to preserve the core ranch as an example of early pioneer development along the Colorado Front Range. Several thousand school-age children use the ranch as a laboratory for environmentally oriented field trips. These excursions also afford first-hand acquaintance with the historical heritage of a relatively unblemished pioneer homestead.

MacGregor Ranch is a testament to human endeavor in a once wild land. The MacGregor legacy speaks to future generations of visitors to Estes Park. The last ranch house has been turned into a museum, workhorses have been purchased to operate the old farm machinery, cattle graze in the meadows. The Black Canyon ranch spanning three generations of MacGregors flourishes.[95]

James R. Riley Jr., the former Colorado assistant attorney general who together with colleague Howard Kenison worked to save the ranch from sale, said it well:

It's not just the trees, the dirt and the buildings at MacGregor Ranch being saved. . . . it's something very special that affects the mind, and the way we live and appreciate life. It's not just this unique natural beauty, but a genesis for minds and people and educational concepts, and a realization of the true potential.

That's what Orpha Kendall, other volunteers and all of us are working for, so that people go forth from MacGregor and actively work to protect the values we see and cherish in the 1873 homestead ranch. That's the end of the rainbow.[96]

The MacGregor Ranch museum offers visitors a chance to sample western ranch life of days past. (Mary Ann Kressig)

Notes

1. Sylvia K. Burack, ed., *The Writer's Handbook* (Boston: The Writer Inc., 1991), 253-54.

2. The author was startled to discover the anonymous "Overland Correspondent" columns in the *Black Earth Advertiser*. The unsigned letters appeared to be sent from the same locations as the letters MacGregor Ranch had in its possession written from Alva Adams to his childhood sweetheart, Clara Heeney, during that same period of time. It seemed unusual that when the weekly issues of the *Advertiser* carried news items about the Adams family or its whereabouts, the paper avoided publishing Dane's articles. It also seemed unlikely that there could be another person sending articles for the newspaper from identical locations, as in 1870, Black Earth had a population of only 962 in the township and 320 in the village. Not until getting acquainted with Alva B. Adams III of Pueblo was the author able to prove that Dane was in reality Alva Adams. Alva, in his travel journal now in the possession of his great grandson, confirmed that he was indeed the anonymous Dane. Perhaps Adams, having newly come of age in 1871 and realizing the importance of being in charge of his family's expedition to Colorado, may have chosen anonymity because he preferred to avoid being remembered as a former teenager from Black Earth while promoting his ideas in the *Advertiser*.

3. This collection from the Colorado Historical Society archives is an unpublished work consisting of biographical material, mostly undated, by an unknown author. Along with many items written by Alva Adams are found numerous articles concerning himself, biographical anecdotes and genealogical records of the Adams and Blanchard families over several generations, political material, letters written by his mother to a good friend and recollections of his younger sister, Elizabeth "Libbie." Within this collection are essays by someone who obviously did extensive work, but did not leave his or her name on it. While there is no way to know for sure who was responsible for the collection, we know that this is a very insightful analysis written by someone who knew quite a lot about Alva Adams and his family. Great-grandson Alva B. Adams of Pueblo feels that it was his grandmother, Mrs. Alva B. Adams, the former Elizabeth Matty of Denver, to whom we should largely be indebted for this work.

4. This combination lumber office and home was built two months before the October 10, 1871, *Rocky Mountain News* carried a story describing a second structure 24 feet by 80 feet Alva was building nearby, setting up shop for the Sanborn

and Adams lumberyard. By the time Alva was putting up this second building, there were more than 100 people and some 50 houses, shanties and tents in Colorado Springs. William N. Byers, *Encyclopedia of Biography of Colorado: History of Colorado* (Chicago: The Century Publishing and Engraving Company, 1901), 201; *Sketches of Colorado Vol. 1* (Denver: Western Press Bureau Company, 1911), 76-77; *Colorado Heritage,* Winter, 1993, 37; John Wagner, "A queer embryo-looking place it is . . . ." (with sketch map of Colorado Springs, 1872), *Gazette-Telegraph*, November 18, 1990), 1-8. In the fourth volume of his edition of Hall's *History of Colorado*, Alva Adams wrote this footnote: "The first completed house on the present site of Colorado Springs was the one-story office built by Alva Adams, who was in the employ of C.W. Sanborn. It was designed and used as a lumberyard office and was finished August 7, 1871." Adams Collection #2, FF 5, Ch. 4, 30.

5. "Old Days," *Madison: Capital Times*, January 18, 1934.

6. John Adams was a member of the Wisconsin Legislature from 1868 to 1870, served as sheriff of Dane County from 1874-1875 and was elected to the state senate in 1882.

7. Letter from Virgil Matz, research historian, Mazomanie Historical Society.

8. Adams Collection #2, FF 39, Ch. 1, 2-3, 5, 7-8.

9. A new museum building reopened in June, 1969.

10. In her October 2, 1870, letter to her friend, Eliza wrote, "Alva has been sick since he graduated." Adams Collection #2, FF 74, letters from Eliza Adams to Mary McNatt Barnes.

11. In 1845, while Wisconsin was still a territory, a free school was organized at Kenosha. When Wisconsin was admitted to the union in 1848, the new state constitution made provisions for creating free common schools to be supported by taxes from five different sources. In 1856, Wisconsin won recognition for establishing the nation's first kindergarten, at Watertown. Mrs. Carl Schurz began this school with German-speaking children of that area in attendance. Svea M. Adolphson, *A History of Albion Academy 1853-1918* (Beloit, Wisconsin: Rock County Rehabilitation Services Inc., 1976), 1-3, 5.

12. Alva's older brother, Charles, who died in 1870 at age 22, always was sickly. Presumably, that is why he did not attend the academy. Younger brother George also was sickly, and there is no record that he or any of the other Adams children attended an academy.

13. Alva referred to his education as "common school" in a letter to the Knickerbocker Publishing Company, November 28, 1902, in reply to a request for biographical information. His letterhead was that of "The Pueblo Savings Bank, Alva Adams, President." State Historical Society of Wisconsin Archives Reading Room.

14. This information was received in the September 27, 1989, letter from the Wisconsin Alumni Association, Jennette Poulik, membership assistant.

15. Years later, University President Edward Birge delighted in suggesting that the "Ladies Hall" dormitory built during Chadbourne's administration be renamed Chadbourne Hall in honor of the president who most bitterly opposed coeducation.

16. The school was prosperous and gave general satisfaction, but Miss Mortimer was oppressed with responsibilities. She sought to share these responsibilities with other teachers, who were faithful and efficient, but the lease made her alone responsible to the trustees and the public both for the character of the school and its financial success, and she was more and more convinced that this was not the proper system under which to conduct a school. Clara's 1870-71 diary, October 29, 1870; William W. Wight, *Annals of a Milwaukee College 1848-1891*, 32. See also Minerva Brace Norton, *A True Teacher: Mary Mortimer, a Memoir* (New York: F.H. Revell Company, c. 1875).

17. The 1880 Census for Estes Park, precincts 6 and 9, Larimer County, June 18, 19, 21-24, was recorded by the Reverend W.H. McCreery, a young circuit-riding missionary from Pennsylvania who came to Estes Park in 1875.

18. Adams Collection #2, FF 39, Ch. 3, 21.

19. Alva's personal travel journal of the family's covered wagon trip is now in the possession of his great grandson, Alva B. Adams III of Pueblo.

20. *Kansas Weekly Tribune*, October 12, 1865, 97, as reported by the *Kansas Historical Quarterly*, Vol XVII, May, 1919, No. 2, 97.

21. Dr. Samuel Edwin Solly, an English doctor who came to Colorado Springs in search of a cure for his tuberculosis and remained to found several sanitaria in the Pikes Peak region, wrote in 1880, "It is often estimated that a third of the population of Colorado came for their health or that of their families, and probably the estimate is not excessive."

22. *Trails West* (Washington, D.C.: National Geographic Society, 1979), inside book jacket, front.

23. Richard M. Ketchum, introduction, *The American Heritage Book of the Pioneer Spirit* (New York: American Heritage Publishing Company Inc. 1959), 7.

24. Adams Collection #2, FF 39, Ch. 3, 26.

25. Adams Collection #2, FF 41, Ch. 15, 121.

26. John D. Unruh Jr., *The Plains Across* (Urbana: University of Illinois Press, 1982), 134, 39. The last of the Indian uprisings in Colorado took place in the summer of 1887, "when the young stripling who had put up the first rude 'office building' in Colorado Springs had become Governor of the State of Colorado."

27. Adams Collection #2, FF 40, 75-76, reference to Vol. 1, *History of Woman's Suffrage*, 722.

28. Joanna L. Stratton, *Pioneer Women: Voices from the Kansas Frontier* (New York: Simon and Schuster, 1981), 57.

29. Editors of American Heritage, *The American Heritage Book of the Pioneer Spirit* (New York: American Heritage Publishing Company, 1959), 264.

30. Adams Collection #2, FF 4, Ch. 3, 27.

31. The *Colorado Springs Gazette*, July 31, 1921.

32. *Portrait and Biographical Record of the State of Colorado* (Chicago: Chapman Publishing Company, 1899), 295 (courtesy City of Greeley Museums).

33. E.O. Davis, *The First Five Years of the Railroad Era in Colorado* (Golden: Sage Books Inc., 1948), 163.

34. Ed. C. Starrett & L.A. Snyder, publishers, *Pioneer Edition,* the *El Paso County Democrat,* December, 1908, 3.

35. Robert G. Athearn, "The Denver and Rio Grande Railway," *Colorado Magazine,* January, 1958, 44.

36. Considering Alva's recent illness, his climbing of Pikes Peak was a remarkable feat. Today's hardiest visitors climb to the 14,110-foot summit over an 11.7- mile trail that is an immense improvement over the route taken by Alva and his party on their wilderness climb. There are now modern concessions and souvenir stands at the top of the peak and visitors reach the summit by road or cog railway. But to this day, anyone with a history of cardiac or respiratory problems is advised not to make the trip to the summit.

37. Although Clara's name on her wedding announcement of December 25, 1873, was spelled "Mariae Clara" and her first name was sometimes written as "Maria," Clara spelled her name "Marie Clara" when she signed her last will and testament on December 23, 1899.

38. Adams Collection #2, Ch. 3, 26-28.

39. Classmates and friends wrote messages, some humorous, many sentimental, in Clara's autograph album beginning in 1869. Clara stopped collecting autographs after meeting Alex MacGregor. His message, written in Denver on April 20, 1873, reads "Tengo la honra de ser vuestra amigo." This was the identical message he wrote on the small 1873 greeting card, the size of a place card, that Clara received after she and her mother returned to Black Earth.

40. "The pictorial record of the west," *Kansas Historical Quarterly,* May, 1949, 100. Mention of the Ford, Gookins and Elkins party also was made in the daily *Rocky*

Mountain News on September 3, 8, 22, 27, 1866.

41. Isabella L. Bird, *A Lady's Life in the Rocky Mountains* (Norman: University of Oklahoma Press, 1960), 74.

42. Clara painted the Monominee River in Milwaukee in August, 1872. In September, she produced the Platte River "forty miles from Denver" and the Platte Mountains Ranch on the Platte River "seventy miles from distant Snowy Range," now known as the Mummy Range. In October, she painted the gateway to the Garden of the Gods with Pikes Peak in the distance. Her western collection from the Colorado Springs vicinity also included Cheyenne Mountain from the Garden of the Gods and Lake George. Not one of these scenes depicted any area near Estes Park.

43. The 1877 date of death was the clue that helped reveal Alexander's heritage. In his diary written during that year, Alex mentioned a letter from a cousin concerning his grandfather's will, and made reference to two of his aunts, listing one by her husband's name, (Jedidiah) Hyde. These were daughters of Duncan Jr. and sisters of Alex's father, Alexander.

44. The genealogy was determined through study of the MacGregor diaries and comparing them with information furnished through the courtesy of the Vermont Historical Society; Joseph C. Tichy Jr., Whispering Pines, North Carolina, assistant chieftan, Clan Gregor Society; and the sixth Duncan McGregor, Duncan Bruce McGregor of Gibbon, Nebraska, son of Duncan Earl McGregor, born in Alburg, Vermont.

45. When the proprietor of the *Mirror*, Daniel H. Sumner, was about 30 years of age, he had taken up the study of law, reading for a time in the office of a Michigan senator. Another report stated that he had prepared himself for his chosen profession with a course of reading at Kalamazoo. Sumner was admitted to the Michigan Bar in 1868. He moved to Wisconsin and opened a law office at Oconomowoc the same year, or the fall of the following year. A year or two later, he opened an office in Waukesha, Wisconsin. Being in poor health, he was unable to practice when he first came to Wisconsin; most of his time was spent at Oconomowoc as co-proprietor of the *La Belle Mirror*. Sumner moved his law practice to Waukesha in 1870, served as Waukesha County district attorney from 1875 to 1877, and served in the U.S. Congress. After his stay in Washington, he continued his law practice in Waukesha. Sumner's wife, whom he married in 1877, later studied law with her husband and for years was associated with him in practice. In December of 1880, she was admitted to the bar as an active practitioner, making her the only woman member of the Waukesha County Bar. This reinforces the likelihood that MacGregor studied law with Sumner, his co-publisher.

46. About the year 1872, Alex was clerk of the Arapahoe County court, presided over by Judge Clough.

47. The Honorable Henry P.H. Bromwell came to Denver from Illinois in 1870. He was a Republican, an attorney, judge, congressman as well as a member of the territorial council of 1874 and the legislature of 1879. At one time, he was connected with the Odd Fellows. He was said to be "A man who had in him something of the Spartan spirit." For a third of a century, he was one of Denver's foremost citizens. Wilbur Fisk Stone, *History of Colorado* (Chicago: The S.J. Clarke Publishing Company, 1981), 888.

48. Undoubtedly, this was the Rev. M.M. Martin, who served congregations in both the Black Earth and the Mazomanie Congregational churches.

49. Alex was appointed by Governor John L. Routt, last territorial governor and first state governor of Colorado.

50. Duane A. Smith, *Rocky Mountain West* (Albuquerque: University of New Mexico Press, 1992), 79. Smith's exact reference: Frank Fossett, Colorado . . . *(Denver: Daily Tribune* Steam Printing House, 1876), 144-45, 147, 438, 467.

51. Clare Arthur, *The MacGregors and Black Canyon Ranch: Three Generations of Tradition* (Estes Park: Rocky Mountain National Park, 1984), 1.

52. Reprinted in the *New Lyons Recorder*, XIX, No. 40, July 9, 1987, 6.

53. "Evans of Estes Park," *Rocky Mountain News,* August 26, 1874, 4.

54. Burlington, a settlement on the south bank of the St. Vrain River, was the forerunner of Longmont, which was settled in 1871. In 1873, the Burlington post office was moved north to Longmont.

55. Dorothy Large, ed., *As We Were: Life in Early Longmont 1871-1900 as Reflected in the Newspapers of the Day* (Longmont: Sharer Books, 1977), 4.

56. Bird, 73, 111, 118.

57. Pat Barr, *A Curious Life for a Lady* (New York: Ballantine Books, 1972).

58. Bird, 80-81.

59. Bird, 110.

60. Dave Hicks, *Estes Park from the Beginning* (Denver: Egan Print Company in association with A-T-P Publishing Company, 1976), 12.

61. James H. Pickering, editor, *Frederick Chapin's Colorado: The Peaks About Estes Park and Other Writings* (Niwot: University Press of Colorado, 1995), 3-4.

62. Rev. E.J. Lamb, *Miscellaneous Meditations: Estes Park 1871-1921* (South Bend, Indiana: The Publisher's Press Room and Bindery Company n.d.), 129-30.

63. Louisa Ward Arps, "Letters from Isabella Bird," *Colorado Quarterly*, Summer 1955, 27.

64. C.W. Buchholtz, *Rocky Mountain National Park: A History* (Boulder: Colorado Associated University Press, 1983), 69.

65. Abner E. Sprague, "The Estes and Rocky Mountain National Parks," *Estes Park Trail*, May 12, 1922, 3.

66. Louisa Ward Arps and Elinor Eppich Kingery, *High Country Names: Rocky Mountain National Park* (Estes Park: Rocky Mountain Nature Association, 1972), 108. "Rocky Mountain Jim may yet take his place in history as the rugged American hero of Estes Park."

67. Ruth Stauffer, *This was Estes Park* (Estes Park: Estes Park Area Historical Museum, 1976), 14.

68. James H. Pickering, *This Blue Hollow: The Annals of Estes Park: A Colorado Reader* (unpublished), 35.

69. Arps, 41.

70. Pickering, ed., *Frederick Chapin's Colorado: The Peaks About Estes Park and Other Writings*, 3-4.

71. Ibid.

72. June E. Carothers, *Estes Park Past and Present* (Denver: The University of Denver Press, 1951), 57.

73. Lindsley & Parker, druggists, were located at 270 Fifteenth, Denver.

74. Dee Brown, *The Gentle Tamers: Women of the Old Wild West* (Lincoln and London: University of Nebraska Press, 1981), 203.

75. Sprague, *Estes Park Trail*, April 20, 1923, 3.

76. Adams Collection #2, FF 39, Ch. 1, 2.

77. Brown, 201.

78. Everett Dick, *The Sod-House Frontier* (Lincoln: Johnsen Publishing Company, 1954), 238-39.

79. Stephen J. Leonard, Thomas J. Noel, *Denver: Mining Camp to Metropolis* (Niwot: University Press of Colorado, 1990), 51.

80. The date of birth given on Halbert's college entrance records was 1887. According to his death certificate, he was born in 1886.

81. Arthur, 10-11.

82. *Portrait and Biographical Record of the State of Colorado,* 1898, 114-16.

83. Arthur, 11.

84. Ibid.

85. An example of Alex's North Park claims included one filed in 1879 for the Mary Lode, a quartz mine, registered in Grand County, State of Colorado.

86. This quotation is from a printed memorial tribute to Alva, "Alva Adams," by J.F. Keating. Adams was a friend of the grandfather of Estes Park resident Doris Dillon and her brother, Joe Dillon, Seattle. Their mother was a Galligan, and lived about a block from the Adams' brick mansion.

87. James H. Pickering, *Joe Mills, Mountain Boyhood* (Lincoln and London: University of Nebraska Press, 1988), 9-10.

88. Arps, Kingery, 130.

89. Forward by Tom Danton, *Enos A. Mills, Adventures of a Nature Guide & Essays in Interpretations* (Friendship WI: New Past Press Inc., 1990), 10.

90. Buchholtz, 104.

91. Letter from Ferril Atkins, November 11, 1993.

92. Fielder, Barron & Mills, *Rocky Mountain National Park: A 100 Year Perspective* (Denver: Westcliffe Publishers, n.d., c. 1995), 8.

93. Long Hoefts Architects, *Architectural Assessment: MacGregor Ranch Museum,* December, 1993, 1, 4.

94. Joanne Ditmer, "A Ranch Where the Good Folks Won," *The Denver Post,* 4D, September 13, 1992.

95. Harriet Burgess, *History of Larimer County, Vol. 1* (Boulder: Norlin Library Archives, University of Colorado), 289-290.

96. Joanne Ditmer, *Empire Magazine, The Denver Post,* October 28, 1979, 16.

Index